RENEE
MONTGOMERY

**NATIONAL GEOGRAPHIC KiDS**

**ESPN**

# IT'S A NUMBERS GAME!

# BASKETBALL

The math behind the *perfect bounce pass,* **the buzzer-beating bank shot,** and *so much more!*

James Buckley, Jr.

Foreword by **NBA Superstar** KOBE BRYANT

NATIONAL GEOGRAPHIC
WASHINGTON, D.C.

# TABLE OF CONTENTS 1

The numbers in this book reflect the 2018–2019 NCAA season, the 2018 WNBA season, and the 2018–2019 NBA season, unless otherwise noted.

**W**hen it came to school, I was an English guy. Reading stories, writing stories, telling elaborate fictitious stories in front of the class. But when it comes to basketball, I'm all about the numbers.

How many shots have I made on the way to my goal of hitting 500 in practice? How many free throws can I make in a row? What's the score and how many points are we up by? What's the geometric angle of the arc as the ball heads toward the rim? What degree does my foot need to be pointing out to give me the best pivot?

Success is in the detail—and the detail is in the math.

Players use it to improve their game, and analysts and coaches use it to keep track of who's at the top of their game. Any time you make a bounce pass or compare your team's score to the opposing team, you're using math.

*It's a Numbers Game: Basketball* explains all the numbers behind the sport to give you a better understanding of the game, and even improve your own play on the court. You'll learn about geometry, physics, and statistics, but you'll also read about some of the greatest plays in basketball history and the awesome athletes behind the jersey numbers that made those plays happen. Speaking of awesome, did you know my basketball muse, Bill Russell, has 11 championship rings? Eleven!

The idea is to make math as fun as the game itself. Next time you play, challenge yourself by keeping track of your shots, your score, your friends' scores. Or, check out this book's activities and create your own heat map to see where you perform best on the court.

Whether you're a basketball newbie, you play on your school's team, or you're just a hoop-head who loves watching the game and keeping track of your favorite players, you've got it all in this book.

Always remember, when curiosity strikes and you need help with the game ... just check the numbers.

**Kobe Bryant**

KOBE BRYANT OF THE LOS ANGELES LAKERS DRIBBLES THE BALL DURING A GAME AGAINST THE NEW YORK KNICKS IN 2011.

# CHAPTER ONE

# ON THE CO

# OURT!

**B**asketball can be played on different surfaces, from wood to asphalt to concrete. Games have also taken place on dirt courts, sand courts, brick courts, and even a court on the deck of an aircraft carrier! From the lines on the ground to the hoops in the air, here's a numbers-packed look at the place where the game is played.

## STAT STORY

To make a brand-new wood floor for the 2017 NCAA men's Final Four (the finals of an annual U.S. college basketball tournament), a company needed 500 trees. It carved these trees into 418 panels of wood. Laid end to end, the panels would have covered 10 miles (16 km)! It took nearly 3,500 hours for workers to get the wood ready for the arena. When it was laid out, the court covered 9,800 square feet (910 sq m).

# FULL SIZE

You don't need a full court to play hoops, but it is nice! Full-size courts are 94 feet (28.7 m) long and 50 feet (15.2 m) wide. The first court ever used for the game was much smaller. That's because James Naismith, the inventor of basketball, only had a gym that was 54 feet (16.5 m) long. Naismith made up basketball in one day (really!) in 1891. He was a busy gym teacher in Springfield, Massachusetts, U.S.A., looking for a new way to keep his college-age students busy on a winter's day. The game of basketball was born. Check out the diagram below for other key court numbers.

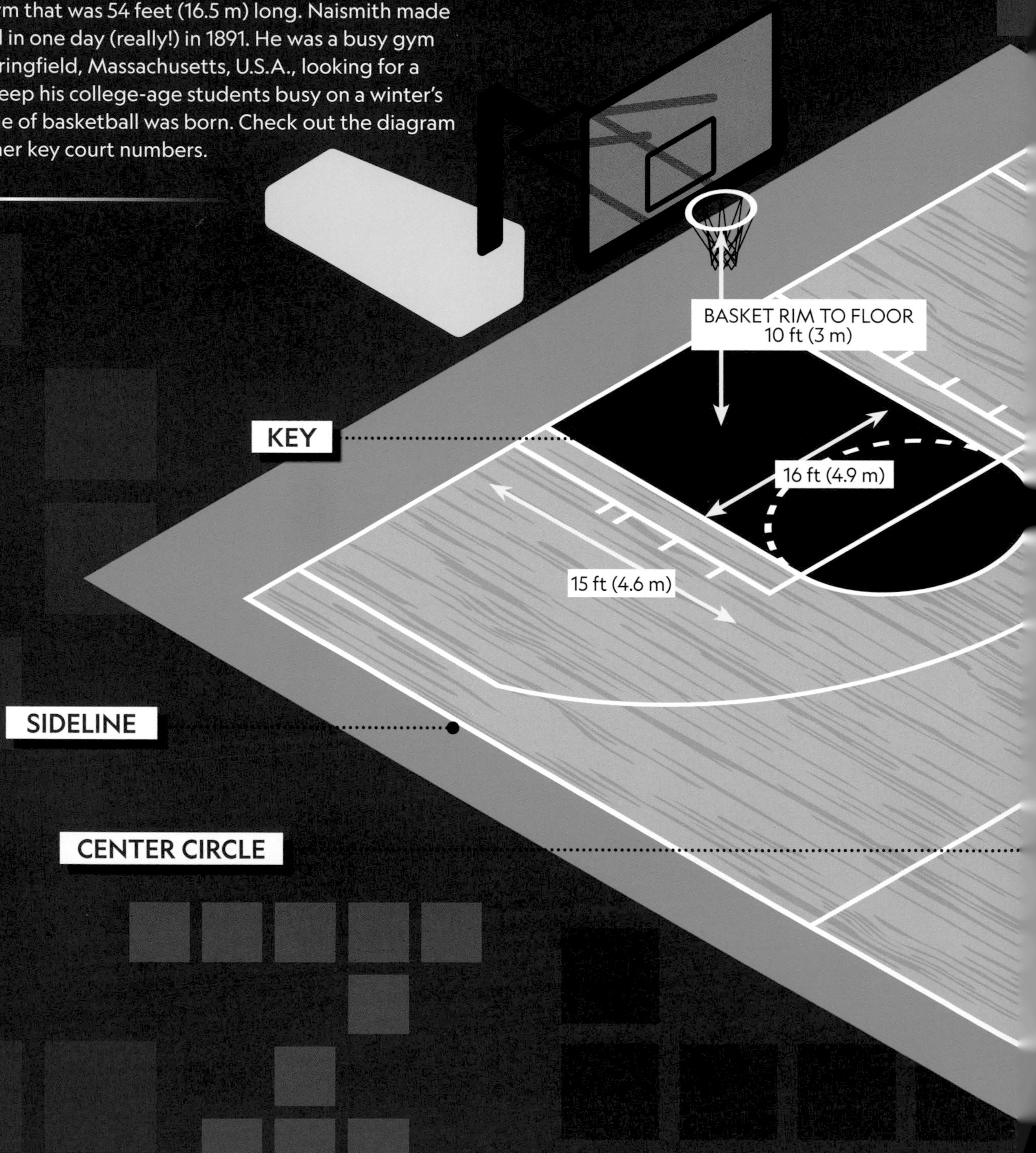

BASKET RIM TO FLOOR
10 ft (3 m)

KEY

16 ft (4.9 m)

15 ft (4.6 m)

SIDELINE

CENTER CIRCLE

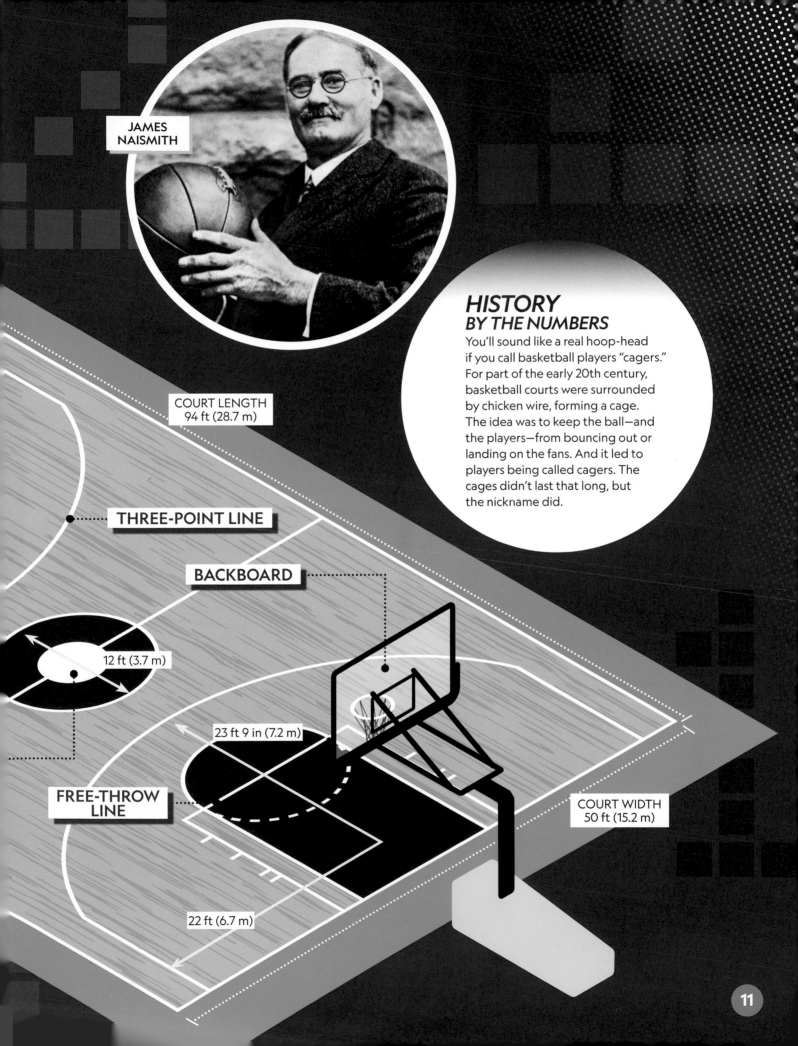

JAMES NAISMITH

COURT LENGTH
94 ft (28.7 m)

## HISTORY
### BY THE NUMBERS
You'll sound like a real hoop-head if you call basketball players "cagers." For part of the early 20th century, basketball courts were surrounded by chicken wire, forming a cage. The idea was to keep the ball—and the players—from bouncing out or landing on the fans. And it led to players being called cagers. The cages didn't last that long, but the nickname did.

THREE-POINT LINE

BACKBOARD

12 ft (3.7 m)

23 ft 9 in (7.2 m)

FREE-THROW
LINE

COURT WIDTH
50 ft (15.2 m)

22 ft (6.7 m)

# THE KEY TO THE COURT

In basketball, the key isn't a piece of metal like what you use to lock your house, but rather a rectangular area with a circle at one end inside the free-throw lane beneath each basket. It's where a lot of the slam-bang action is, with players' bodies often crashing into and around each other. Controlling the key is a big part of the game. Players on offense are taught to "box out" an opponent in the key by putting their bodies between the opponent and the basket. The idea is to get into a better place to make a rebound of a missed shot. Players on defense face out and try to prevent opponents from cruising through the key to the hoop.

## WHY "KEY"?

Why not "box"? Take a look at this picture of a key on a 1956 basketball court. The center area was narrower than it is today, once measuring only six feet (1.8 m) wide before expanding in 1964 to 16 feet (4.9 m). What did it look like back in the day? OK, it looked kind of like a thumb drive. But they didn't have those 70 years ago. People nicknamed it after another object it resembles—a keyhole.

**THE NEW YORK KNICKS BATTLE FOR THE REBOUND WITH THE MINNEAPOLIS LAKERS.**

## DIGIT-YOU-KNOW?

The key is the area nearest to the basket, and the point of the game is to put the ball into the basket. So, wouldn't it be a good idea to just camp out in the key and wait for the ball? Well, yes, but that would give you an unfair advantage. That's why the three-second rule was invented. A player on offense can't be in the key for more than three seconds in a row while his or her team has the ball. You can go in and out, cross it, and, of course, drive in and shoot. But you can't stand there for more than three seconds. Keep your feet moving!

## STAT STORY

Basketball games played in other countries once used a wider key. The area was in the shape of a trapezoid, not a rectangle. It was 12 feet (3.7 m) wide at the free-throw lane. Under the basket, however, the key expanded to 19.7 feet (6 m). In 2010, the key in these countries was changed to be similar to the standard measurements used by the NBA so that the rules would be the same everywhere.

# ONE... TWO... THREE POINTS!

**S**o, we've got a ball and a court. Now, let's start putting the ball into the basket. After all, getting more points than the other team is the whole point of the game! Here are the leading numbers when it comes to scoring baskets.

SHAQUILLE HARRISON

**1** This is the number of points a team gets for a free throw, a shot awarded to a team that has been fouled against. A foul is when a player breaks the rules of the game. During a free throw, a player stands 15 feet (4.6 m) from the backboard and no one gets to guard him or her (it's free ... remember?). A very good pro player should make about 8 of every 10 free throws.

**2** Any shot taken from the area inside the three-point arc (see graphic at right) is worth two points. All these successful shots are called field goals (FGs). Yep, the same term is used in football. That sport used it first, so Naismith borrowed it when he invented his game. However, in the first basketball games, a field goal was worth only one point!

MARCUS MORRIS

CHARLES MATTHEWS

**3** Here's the newest member to the family of basketball numbers. Until 1967, a field goal from *anywhere* on the court was just a deuce (fancy word alert—that's a basketball term meaning "two"). When the American Basketball Association (ABA) was formed in 1967, 21 years after the formation of the NBA in 1946, the new league thought a three-point shot would get a lot of attention. The ABA was right. Fans loved the long buckets made behind a designated line. In 1976, the ABA merged with the NBA and the three-point shot went away because it wasn't part of the NBA game. But in 1979, the NBA began awarding three points for shots taken beyond the three-point arc, just like the ABA had. College hoops and high school ball quickly followed. The game has not been the same since. Offenses changed to take advantage of the higher-scoring shot. Players began to improve their long-range shooting. Today, most fans can't imagine basketball without the three-pointer.

# HOW FAR IS A *THREE-POINT SHOT?*

It depends on which league you play in. This graphic shows the different arc distances by league. As long as a player's feet are behind this line when the shot is taken—and the ball goes into the basket—it's a trey (yes, a fancy word for three).

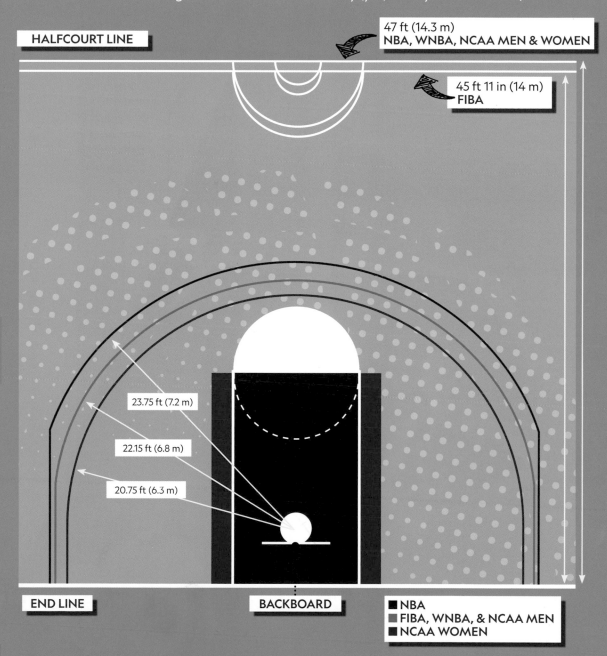

HALFCOURT LINE

47 ft (14.3 m)
NBA, WNBA, NCAA MEN & WOMEN

45 ft 11 in (14 m)
FIBA

23.75 ft (7.2 m)

22.15 ft (6.8 m)

20.75 ft (6.3 m)

END LINE

BACKBOARD

- ■ NBA
- ■ FIBA, WNBA, & NCAA MEN
- ■ NCAA WOMEN

## DIGIT-YOU-KNOW?

Basketball's three-point shot has been a big hit; so why not a four-point shot? In 2017, the rapper and actor Ice Cube helped start a three-on-three pro hoops league called BIG3. To spice things up for the fans, the league added three special spots on its half-court, 30 feet (9.1 m) from the hoop. A shot from inside each spot is worth four points! Ricky Davis, Baron Davis, David Hawkins, and Nate Robinson all made four four-pointers in the 2018 season, tying for the lead.

# THE *HOOP*

Remember James Naismith, the inventor of basketball? An elevated running track looped around the walls of his gym at the YMCA International Training School (now Springfield College) in Springfield, Massachusetts. The bottom of the track was 10 feet (3 m) above the gym floor. That's where he nailed up two peach baskets to serve as the goals for his new sport. Basketball baskets have been 10 feet (3 m) above the ground ever since.

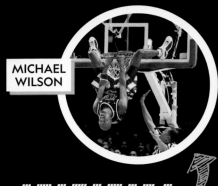

MICHAEL WILSON

## STATSTARS

It's a bird, it's a plane, it's a ... basketball player? Former Harlem Globetrotters star Michael Wilson set a world record in April 2000 for highest dunk when he soared into the air and dunked a ball through a rim 12 feet (3.7 m) off the ground!

Basketball Basket
**10 FT (3 M)**

Check out how these basketball legends (including you!) measure up to the height of a basketball hoop.

**7 FT 7 IN (2.3 M)**

**6 FT 8 IN (2 M)**

**5 FT 10 IN (1.8 M)**

**4 FT 8 IN (1.4 M)**

Manute Bol

LeBron James

James Naismith

A 10-year-old

# COURT *WORLD!*

Basketball courts are always packed with action—they can also be packed with trivia!

### World's Oldest Court

Naismith was teaching students at the YMCA International Training School when he invented basketball in the late 19th century. The game spread quickly through a worldwide network of YMCA gymnasiums. One wood-floor YMCA gym in Paris, France, has been the site of hoops games since 1893. It claims to be the world's oldest court still in use.

### World's Highest Court

Lhasa, Tibet, is one of the world's highest cities, located in the Himalayan region of Asia. The city is home to the world's highest basketball court, which sits more than 12,000 feet (3,658 m) above sea level. Talk about being at the top of your game!

### The Floating Court

In the past, the NCAA men's basketball season has tipped off with a special game to honor and thank the U.S. military. In 2011, a court was set up in an unusual place: on the deck of an aircraft carrier! Along with sports drinks and tape for wrapping ankles, team trainers probably had to pack seasickness medicine!

# TRY *THIS!*

## How far can you shoot a basketball?
Grab a ball and your tape measure and find out.

### What you will need:
- Basketball
- Tape measure
- Basketball hoop
- Painter's tape for an indoor court
- Chalk for an outdoor court

## Steps:

**1** Start by measuring **15 feet** (4.6 m) from the backboard and mark the spot with painter's tape or chalk, depending on where your hoop is. That's the distance of the free-throw line. How many shots can you make from there? What is your longest streak of success?

**2** Measure and mark **24 feet** (7.3 m) from the hoop. Can you make a basket from that distance? That's about the NBA three-point line.

**3** Measure and mark **47 feet** (14.3 m) from the hoop. You're at half-court of an NBA arena. Wow, that basket is far away! Give it a shot!

**4** After shooting from all these distances, begin again at the free-throw line. Start shooting and then take a step back after each shot. From how many steps back can you make a basket?

**5** Once you have set your personal record, get your friends to try. Do you have any hoop heroes in your group?

### DIGIT-YOU-KNOW?
The longest shot ever made in the NBA was a stunning 89 feet (27.1 m). Baron Davis of the Charlotte Hornets made the long-distance heave as the third quarter ended in a 2001 game.

# TIPS

You can shoot a ball any way you want. The pros shoot from over their heads as they jump. For long shots, though, try some other methods. Throwing it underhand gives you a big arc and maybe more distance. Why not throw it like a football? Some NBA stars make long passes that way. Or shove it toward the basket with two hands from in front of your chest.

# CHAPTER TWO

# PERFECT TIMING

In basketball, every second counts—and every second is counted. Even *parts* of seconds are counted! A huge part of the sport has to do with timing, from how long a game lasts to how much time a team has to shoot. Get out your stopwatches and timer apps—here's a look at the big-time numbers in basketball timing.

## STAT STORY

Who keeps time at an NBA or WNBA game? Do the referees have stopwatches? Well, no. The refs have enough to do! There are additional officials who act as time-keepers. They are paid by the teams and trained on the rules. One official runs the game clock, while another takes care of the 24-second shot clock (see page 22). Other officials work as scorekeepers to track the stats and the scoreboard.

# HURRY UP AND SHOOT!

If you went to an NBA game in the late 1940s, you might have fallen asleep. From 1891 through the mid-20th century, teams did not have to take a shot when they had the ball. Many teams would get a lead and then just hold on to the ball for minutes at a time. Sometimes teammates would just pass the ball back and forth. Other teams had great dribblers who would evade their opponent's defense. One NBA game ended with the score 19 to 18. These days, that's how many points are scored during a slow *quarter* of a game!

One way to stop a ball-hogging team was to foul it. That's because after the fouled team took the free throw it was awarded, the ball switched sides. It was the only way to get the ball out of a stalling team's hands.

In 1954, Danny Biasone, owner of the Syracuse Nationals (which became the Philadelphia 76ers in 1964), had a better idea. Along with his team's general manager, Leo Ferris, he came up with the shot clock. Under this rule, a team has to make a shot attempt (one that at least hits the rim) within 24 seconds. If not, time is called and the other team takes over the ball. If the shooting team misses its shot but gets the rebound (this is when a player grabs the ball after a missed shot), it can get a "fresh" 24 seconds.

Almost overnight, the NBA got much more exciting. In the NBA's first season (1946–47), teams averaged 67.8 points per game, or ppg. During the first year of the shot clock, that number jumped to 93.1 ppg. Three years later, every NBA team averaged more than 100 points per game.

By the 1961–62 season, NBA teams averaged 118.8 points per game across the league—still the highest ever!

So, when you see an exciting, high-scoring, fast-paced hoops game today, thank Danny Biasone and Leo Ferris.

## STATSTARS

Here are some of the scoring records that NBA teams have put up, thanks in large part to the 24-second clock.

### Highest Average Points per Game for a Season

**Denver Nuggets,**
1981–82

**126.6**

### Most Points in a Game

**Detroit Pistons,**
December 13, 1983

**186**

### Most Points in One Half

**Phoenix Suns,**
November 10, 1990

**107**

# WHY 24?

Of course, because the NBA shot clock was such a big deal, tons of research went into picking the perfect number for it, right? NBA officials probably used supercomputers and worked with NASA scientists to come up with such a precise figure (otherwise, why not 30 seconds?).

Uh … no, not really.

Here's how 24 became the most important timing number in the NBA (and in the WNBA, since the league switched from the 30-second shot clock in 2006). Danny Biasone and Leo Ferris, the guys who thought up the shot clock did some math. They liked games in which teams took a lot of shots because the games were more exciting, so they looked at the stats from games like that. In those games, each team took about 60 shots. So the two men doubled that number to get 120 shots, the total number of shots in an action-packed game. Then they divided 120 by 2,880, the length of a game in seconds. The result was 24 seconds.

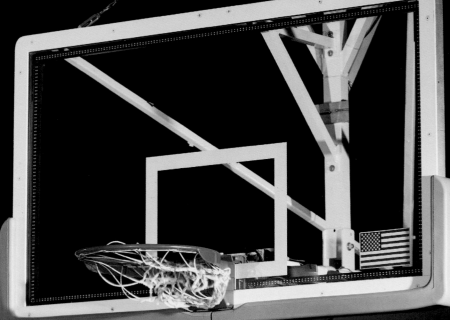

**60** shots
(taken by each team
in a good game)

 **2**
(because there are
two teams, right?)
_____
**120
shots**

 **48** minutes
**in a game**
(the NBA standard
then and now)

 **60** seconds
**in a minute**
(duh)
_____
**2,880
seconds**

**2,880
seconds**

 **120
shots**
_____
**24!**

# TICK TICK TICK

So how long does a basketball game last? That depends on who's playing, where they're playing, and how old the players are. Check out where your favorite league fits on this chart. We've also included the timing of the shot clock for each league.

| LEAGUE | FULL GAME | GAME PARTS | SHOT CLOCK |
|---|---|---|---|
| NBA | 48 minutes | 4 12-minute quarters | 24 seconds |
| WNBA | 40 minutes | 4 10-minute quarters | 24 seconds |
| NCAA men's | 40 minutes | 2 20-minute halves | 30 seconds |
| NCAA women's | 40 minutes | 4 10-minute quarters | 30 seconds |
| FIBA* | 40 minutes | 4 10-minute quarters | 24 seconds |
| High school (U.S.) | 32 minutes | 4 8-minute quarters | None** |

CANDACE PARKER

* Also known as the International Basketball Federation, the organizer of games played between countries

** Controversy! The National Federation of State High School Associations Basketball Rules Committee, which makes rules for high school hoops, says, "No shot clock!" However, eight U.S. states use a 30- or 35-second clock for high school basketball games. And because they use a clock, these states can't take part in national meetings about high school basketball rules. This might change in the future, so watch the clock.

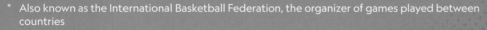

# TIMEOUTS

Can you stop time? No, but you can stop the clock at a hoops game. To do this, coaches and players call a timeout, or TO. Teams use this short pause to catch their breath and call new plays. Some coaches send in new players during timeouts. Others set up a last-second shot. Each level of basketball has its own rules about how many timeouts are allowed. Here's how timeouts work in the WNBA and NBA (starting with the 2017–18 season).

- WNBA: Each timeout lasts 120 seconds.

- NBA: Each timeout lasts 75 seconds.

- WNBA: Each team gets eight timeouts per game.

- NBA: Each team gets seven timeouts per game. (It used to be nine.)

- In the NBA and WNBA, the refs will call at least two timeouts per quarter if neither team calls one. The official reason is to let players rest, but really, it's so TV advertisers can show more commercials!

WNBA HEAD COACH CHERYL REEVE TALKS WITH HER TEAM DURING A TIMEOUT.

TRE'SHAUN FLETCHER CALLS A TIMEOUT.

## COLLEGE TOs

In NCAA men's basketball, each team gets four 75-second timeouts and two 30-second timeouts. In addition, referees can call several timeouts per half for "the media" (again, so TV advertisers can show more commercials). In women's college basketball, there are three 30-second timeouts and a 60-second one, plus media TOs.

## STAT STORY

Players have a lot to do during a game. They have to run, pass, shoot, and play defense. They also need to know how many timeouts their team has. (Because, well, you can't call timeout if you've already run out of them!) In 1993, Chris Webber of the University of Michigan forgot that. In the last seconds of the NCAA Men's Championship game, he tried to call timeout, but there was one problem: Michigan didn't have any left. He was called for a technical foul, the University of North Carolina was awarded two free throws and made them, and Michigan lost the game. Oops.

With all that's going on, miscommunications can happen on the court. In Game 1 of the 2018 NBA Finals, the Cleveland Cavaliers' J. R. Smith grabbed a rebound with just seconds to play. His team was tied with the Golden State Warriors. Later, J. R. said that he thought the Cavs were going to call a timeout. They didn't. J. R. ended up dribbling away the clock and the game went into overtime. If he had shot the ball, his team might have won. In fact, the Cavs ended up losing in overtime!

NBA HEAD COACH DOC RIVERS CALLS A TIMEOUT.

# BUZZER BEATERS

Ever hear of a buzzer-beater? No, that's not someone who jabs on doorbells too hard. A buzzer-beater is a game-winning or game-tying shot that goes in as the game-*ending* buzzer sounds. And there isn't a more exciting play at any level of basketball. Fans rise to their feet, the ball is in the air, the clock ticks to 0.0, then, swish! Cheers! Confetti! Dogpile!

Buzzer-beaters are unique to basketball because no other sport uses a buzzer. (Well, hockey has a horn, but it's not quite the same.) Teams design all sorts of plays when they know they have only a few seconds to make a shot.

Here are just a few of the most famous buzzer-beaters in hoops history.

## 1989 *THE SHOT*

**This was so clutch that people just call it "The Shot." It's Game 5 of the 1989 Eastern Conference first-round playoffs, and Michael Jordan has the ball. His Chicago Bulls were down by a point. Three seconds were left on the clock. No problem. Jordan calmly found an opening, jumped, and shot the ball over Cleveland's Craig Ehlo. Swish! The game was over, the series was over, and Jordan was on his way to becoming a legend.**

## 2004 *NBA WESTERN CONFERENCE SEMIFINALS*

**With a bucket at just 0.9 second until game over during the NBA Western Conference semifinals, Tim Duncan of the San Antonio Spurs put his team in the lead. But that left just enough time for the L.A. Lakers' Derek Fisher to win the game with his own buzzer-beating heave.**

# 2016 NCAA MEN'S FINALS

After the University of North Carolina tied the game with 4.7 seconds left, Villanova quickly brought the ball up the court. Ryan Arcidiacono dribbled a few times. The defense zoomed toward him. He dished the ball to Kris Jenkins (2) who calmly buried a three-point shot as the buzzer went off. Villanova won the championship!

## 2016 WNBA FINALS

The L.A. Sparks were on the road, playing on the home court of the favored Minnesota Lynx. The teams were tied, with time for just one more shot. As the buzzer sounded, Alana Beard of the Sparks nailed a two-pointer. The big win helped the Sparks earn the WNBA title a few games later.

# SECOND BY SECOND

Let's break down one famous recent buzzer-beater, partial second by partial second. The setting is the 2018 NCAA women's national championship game, Notre Dame versus Mississippi State. The score is tied 58–58. Notre Dame finishes a timeout, and the team is about to pass the ball inbounds. The clock will start as soon as a second Notre Dame player touches the ball.

**2.0**
She releases her shot.

**2.2**
Gathering herself, she jumps.

**2.4**
Still dribbling, Ogunbowale nears the sideline.

**2.8**
Ogunbowale dribbles twice; Mississippi State's Victoria Vivians comes over to guard her.

**3.0**
Notre Dame's Arike Ogunbowale gets an inbounds pass from Jackie Young.

THE NOTRE DAME JUNIOR SHOWS OFF PERFECT SHOOTING FORM.

**1.9**
The shot is in the air.

EVERY EYE IN THE PLACE WATCHED OGUNBOWALE'S SHOT.

OGUNBOWALE CELEBRATES HER BUZZER-BEATER WITH A TEAMMATE.

**1.0**
The ball is at the top of its arc toward the hoop.

**0.0**
The ball drops through the basket! Ogunbowale's teammates surround her. Notre Dame wins its first NCAA women's championship since 2001!

**STOPWATCH**

**MODE**

**START/STOP**

**/RESET**

**1:00 27**

# TRY *THIS!*
## Got a stopwatch?
Get ready for some basketball fun. Gather a few friends and take turns timing each other as you try these shots.

### Quick Shot
Have a friend make a pass to you from half-court, as you wait in the key. Turn around and make a shot, then stop the clock. How long did that take? Can you do it in less than three seconds? How about in less than two?

### Length of the Court
Start the clock when you start dribbling at one end of the court. Dribble all the way to the other hoop and make a layup (a short shot dropped into the basket or bounced off the backboard from close range). How long did that take you? Try practicing to see if you can go faster.

## Countdown!

Challenge yourself in this game. Have one friend play defense. The other players count down, starting from 10. Can you make a shot before they get to zero? It's harder when someone's trying to stop you, right?

## Game Time

Play a three-on-three game and have an extra player be the timekeeper. The timekeeper can be your human 24-second clock, making sure that each team takes shots that hit the basketball rim within 24 seconds. The timekeeper can also be the end-of-game buzzer. Decide how long the game will last and then, as it nears the end, the timekeeper can count down to zero. Will you make a buzzer-beater for your team?

## STAT STORY

With 0.3 second or less left on the clock, an NBA or WNBA player is not able to take a game-winning shot from a pass that returns the ball to play after it goes out of bounds. The league passed the rule to make it easier for officials to decide if a shot was taken before the buzzer ending the game went off. A pass can be made toward the basket if the shot doesn't go in and a player tips it in, but teams can't catch a pass and make a shot in 0.3 second or less.

# CHAPTER THREE

# ARE YOU

# A 1 OR A 5?

In the NBA, a basketball team can have 15 players on its roster, or list of players on the team. In the WNBA, there are 12 players on the roster. But no matter what, each team can only have five players on the court. When the ball shoots into the air for a tip-off at the start of a basketball game, 12 or 13 people are on the court. Two or three are referees—they're the ones in a pro game who are usually wearing black and white and are shorter than everyone else on the court. The other 10 folks are, of course, the players—five from each team. In this chapter, we'll look at the players: their positions and what they do, the reasoning behind how their jerseys are numbered, and the ways in which these numbers have changed.

## DIGIT-YOU-KNOW?

Speaking of refs and numbers, did you know that the NBA rule book, which referees must know back to front, is 66 pages long? Or that referees have to know how to do almost 30 different hand signals to call fouls and control the game? In an NBA game, there are three officials: one crew chief, who is the leader of the officials, and two referees.

# NAMING AND NUMBERING THE POSITIONS

For most of the first century of hoops, the five positions on the court were only called by their actual names: guards, center, and forwards. Today, most coaches use numbers to identify the positions. So, instead of being called a plain ol' guard, forward, or center, the positions are usually numbered one through five. These numbers are used in places like play diagrams, where players' numbers are written out on the court instead of their names to show where they need to move for a play. These numbers are separate from the ones on the players' jerseys.

It all seems simple, right? Uh, not quite. Unlike in, say, baseball, in which players tend to remain in their assigned locations, basketball players can find themselves all over the court. They move to where they are needed rather than sticking in one spot. They can also do the jobs of teammates in different positions, depending on where the ball is and what needs to be done to make a play.

Still, there are basic jobs that each position in basketball performs. Check out the positions and numbers in the green boxes that follow before taking a close look at each position's job on the pages ahead.

## HISTORY
### BY THE NUMBERS

Every player on a basketball team plays defense, "guarding" an opponent. So why are only two players known as guards? According to one source, in the early days of hoops, part of each team stayed behind to guard their own basket while the rest of the team moved the ball *forward* and through the *center* to score. So there were actual guards on those teams, and the name stuck even when the game changed several years later to have the whole offensive team move down the court.

GEORGE THOMPSON (25) AND FREDDIE LEWIS (14)

**GUARDS** (TWO PER TEAM): These players play the farthest away from the rest of their teammates, usually shooting from more than just a few feet from their own basket. The two main types of guards today are *point* guards (1) and *shooting* guards (2).

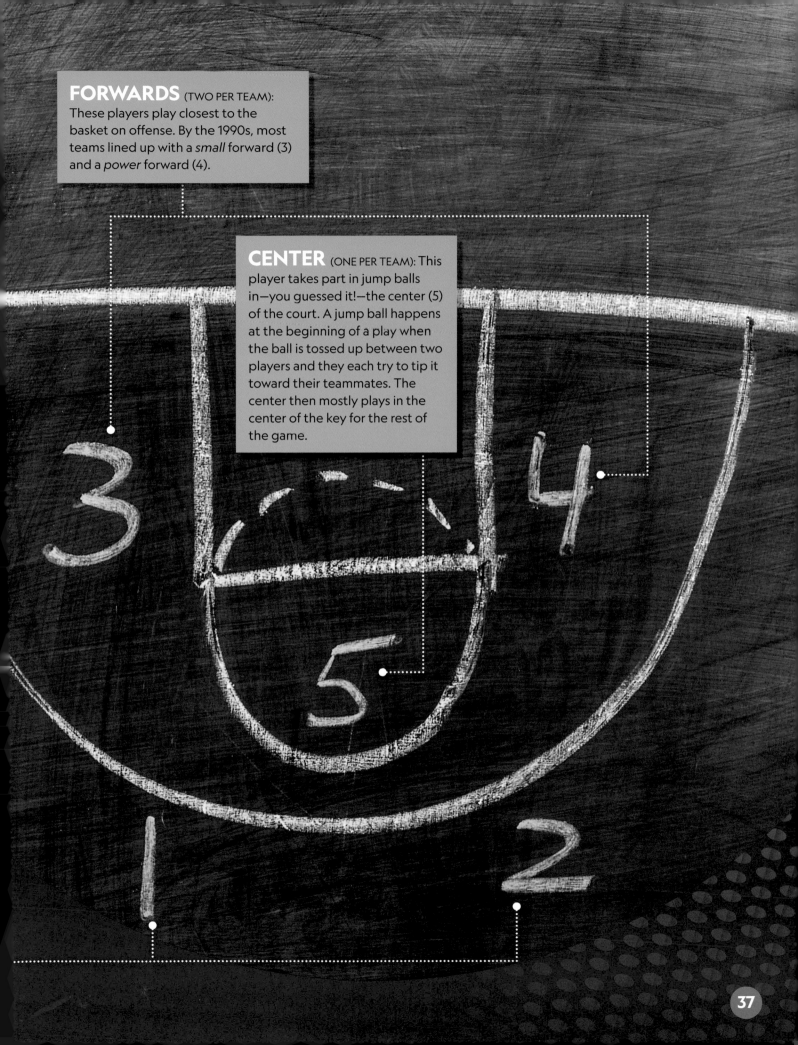

**FORWARDS** (TWO PER TEAM): These players play closest to the basket on offense. By the 1990s, most teams lined up with a *small* forward (3) and a *power* forward (4).

**CENTER** (ONE PER TEAM): This player takes part in jump balls in—you guessed it!—the center (5) of the court. A jump ball happens at the beginning of a play when the ball is tossed up between two players and they each try to tip it toward their teammates. The center then mostly plays in the center of the key for the rest of the game.

# 1 POINT GUARD

Point guards, or number ones, are the playmakers, the commanders on the court. Ones are like quarterbacks in football. The play starts with them. The point guard's job is to take the basketball up the court toward the basket. They sometimes get signals from the coach to run a certain play. And you might see a point guard holding up a number of fingers to signal to teammates which play is coming. (Each team chooses their own numbers to represent different plays.) Then the players all move to their spots, and the action starts!

Ones must be able to dribble and handle the ball well. They can even push past defenders as they dribble. They are experts at finding open teammates and passing the ball to them. Most point guards can also shoot from outside the three-point line with great accuracy. As they bring the ball up the court, they often get a good look at the basket. If they see a shot they like, they take it.

On defense, a point guard has to be superquick because he or she will almost certainly have to stop another point guard from the opposing team.

JUSTIN COBBS, TEAM LE MANS SARTHE, FRANCE

## STATSTARS

There are tons of great point guards in pro basketball, but Stephen "Steph" Curry may be the best. He can sometimes be a two, aka a shooting guard. But his dribbling and passing abilities are too valuable to only let him shoot. In the WNBA, veteran Sue Bird is the league's all-time leader in assists. Passing out assists is a point guard's biggest job.

STEPHEN CURRY

SUE BIRD

## HISTORY
## BY THE NUMBERS

Who is the best point guard of all time? Let the debate begin! Some of the greatest players in NBA history were point guards. But Magic Johnson (an NBA pro between 1979 and 1996) might be at the top of the heap. At 6 feet 9 inches (2 m), he changed people's opinion that really large players couldn't hold the point guard position. He holds the NBA finals record, with 21 assists in a 1984 game. He's also the all-time leader in assists per game, at 11.19. No other player of his size could move the ball like he could—dribbling, passing, and shooting. Since Magic, point guards are expected to be multiskilled.

# 2 SHOOTING GUARD

Score, score, and score some more. That's the shooting guard's responsibility. Shooting guards are typically among the smaller players, so you won't see them crashing the boards, or rebounding, too often. Their job is to nail three-pointers from outside the three-point line, find room for mid-range jumpers in the paint (that is, score on shots taken inside the key), and help the point guard move the ball around the court.

On defense, this position is expected to try to stop the two on the opposing team. That means quick feet, hands up, and hustle, hustle!

One great example of a shooting guard from basketball history? Kobe Bryant. This Los Angeles Lakers legend comes in third for most points scored in the NBA at 33,643 points. That's just below Karl Malone of the Utah Jazz and his 36,928 points, and Kareem Abdul-Jabbar, who holds the record at 38,387 points.

## HISTORY
### BY THE NUMBERS

From 1984 until 2003, Michael Jordan traditionally played the two position. If this position's job is to score, no one did it better. Jordan led the NBA in scoring 10 times during his career and is the NBA's all-time leader in points per game average, at 30.12. Jordan is considered the best shooting guard of all time.

## STATSTARS

In the WNBA, veteran guard Diana Taurasi has scored 8,549 points, more than any other player in league history. Sounds like top shooting guard material for sure! A lot of current players are candidates for the title of top NBA shooting guard. But James Harden is a truly solid pick. The Houston Rockets' NBA MVP for 2017–2018 scored more than 2,000 points that season. Not only can he score, he also sets up his teammates for easy buckets and is a tenacious defender.

KOBE BRYANT

DIANA TAURASI

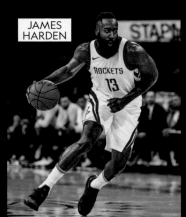
JAMES HARDEN

# 3 SMALL FORWARD

Small forwards have a big job. Their role on the court is to shoot well from a distance, but also to score near the basket. These multitalented players also help with rebounding, and even defend players bigger than they are.

Why is this position called a *small* forward? It's actually unclear where this name came from. What is known is that it has nothing to do with the height of the players. Threes are rarely very small. For instance, Kevin Durant is often listed as a small forward, and he's a whopping 6 feet 10 inches (2.1 m). In fact, most threes are pretty tall, making this an oddly named position.

LEBRON JAMES

## STATSTARS

If you're called "King James," you must be basketball royalty. That's LeBron James's nickname, and he's such a talented player that he plays whichever position he wants. However, he is most often listed as small forward and is considered one of the best threes ever on the court. In the WNBA, we'll name the Minnesota Lynx's small forward Maya Moore as a top three; she's a four-time WNBA champ. Along with that WNBA success, Moore won two NCAA titles with the University of Connecticut, and is a two-time Olympic gold medalist.

### HISTORY BY THE NUMBERS

The great Larry Bird of the Boston Celtics deserves a shout-out as one of history's best small forwards. This famous three could score from anywhere. He was so good that this right-handed player once decided to shoot left-handed during a game, and he still scored 47 points!

KEVIN DURANT

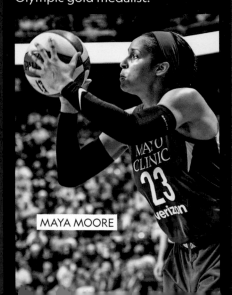

MAYA MOORE

# 4 POWER FORWARD

You want to play as a four? Get ready to work hard. Power forwards, or fours, probably crash into more bodies and take more elbows than any other position does. Their job is to score in the key and get the rebound when they're on defense. They battle under the boards; they clear out space; they push, shove, and scramble for a good position. Fours need to be able to score close to the rim.

On defense, they battle players who match their large size and strength. It's a hardworking position that calls for guts as much as skill.

## HISTORY
## *BY THE NUMBERS*

At 6 feet 11 inches (2.1 m), Tim Duncan was tall enough to play center, a position that requires great height. On most of his teams, he didn't have to because there was another center. That left him as a four, which also requires a large player, and he turned into the best ever, in many experts' opinion. His all-around skills helped him win five NBA titles with the San Antonio Spurs.

## STATSTARS

Candace Parker of the WNBA's Los Angeles Sparks has all the skills to handle the four position at an All-Star level. She has become one of the most dominant players in the league and has guided her team to the playoffs eight times. In the NBA, look no further than Anthony Davis. With long arms, great leaping ability, and under-the-basket intensity, he's become a top power forward in the league.

CANDACE PARKER

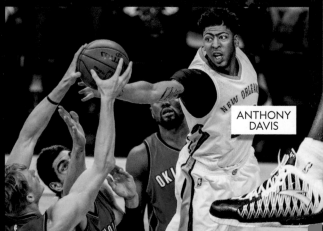

ANTHONY DAVIS

KEVIN GARNETT

SPENCER HAWES

# 5 CENTER

Top basketball players are taller than most of us, but which players also tower above the other players on the court? The centers. At the five spot, look for the tallest player on most teams. The center handles the jump ball, pulls down rebounds, and scores close to the basket. On defense, he or she has to block another center who might be just as tall as they are!

You won't see a lot of fives leading fast breaks, which is when the offense quickly moves the ball up the court after a rebound. They are often the last players back from the defensive end of the court to the offensive end, but they still can get there in time to snag a key rebound. A really great five can dominate a basketball game at both ends of the court. In the NBA, many teams don't have a fixed five. They rotate one of their bigger forwards into the spot as needed.

BRITTNEY GRINER

## HISTORY
### BY THE NUMBERS

The biggest, baddest center in history has to be the Big Fella, Kareem Abdul-Jabbar. He scored 38,387 points in his career, more than any player in NBA history. Between 1969 and 1989, he was a six-time MVP and won six NBA titles with two teams (Milwaukee Bucks and L.A. Lakers). He was smooth but tough and could slam home a dunk.

DEMARCUS COUSINS

## STATSTARS

At 6 feet 9 inches tall (2 m),  Brittney Griner is the top center in her league. She holds the WNBA record for blocks per game, with a 3.17 average. In the NBA, one example of a player who is actually a forward and sometimes plays as a center is DeMarcus (nicknamed "Boogie") Cousins. He's definitely a multitalented player—he once had one of the few 40-point, 20-rebound, 10-assist triple-doubles ever. (Not sure what a triple-double is? Bounce to page 116 to find out.)

# 6 SIXTH PERSON

Why stop at five? In most games, more players take the court than just the five who start for each team. Several other players sit on the bench, ready to be substituted in when needed. The first person off the bench is called the sixth man or woman. This player steps in if the team needs a fresh pair of legs to drive to the basket or a shutdown defender to stop a hot shooter.

Most people who fill this role can score and play defense well. More than anything else, they hustle! When a sixth man or woman comes into the game, they are supposed to energize the team. And oftentimes, this person can change the game!

## DIGIT-YOU-KNOW?

In 2018, Lou Williams of the Los Angeles Clippers became the first "sixth man" to lead his team in average points per game and average assists per game (see page 88). Sounds like Lou should be starting, *not* coming off the bench!

DENNIS SCHRODER

DOMANTAS SABONIS

DEWANNA BONNER

## STAT STORY

The Indiana Pacers are led by superstar Victor Oladipo, But he can't do it all, so the team calls on sixth man Domantas Sabonis, who is one of the most accurate shooters in the NBA. The WNBA gives an annual award to the top sub, called the Sixth Woman of the Year Award. DeWanna Bonner has earned three of these awards and Alli Quigley has earned two.

# NUMBERS ON THEIR BACKS

Basketball has a lot of rules. The reason to have rules such as no kicking the basket ball and no pulling down an opponent's shorts are obvious. Others are not as obvious. For instance, uniform numbers in college ball can't feature the following digits: 6, 7, 8, or 9.

Why? College numbers have to be 5 and below because that's how many fingers referees—and, of course, humans in general—have on each hand.

When an NCAA ref calls a foul on a player, he or she has to tell the official scorer who committed the foul. To do this, the referee signals the official with his or her hands, often using fingers to represent the numerals on the player's uniform. If a uniform had, say, a 9 on it, that could get confusing, because holding up 4 fingers on one hand and 5 on the other could translate to the number 9, the number 45, or the number 54.

The five-and-below rule makes it easier to avoid misunderstandings. The NCAA referee can easily signal permitted numbers such as 3, 42, and 55, using one hand for the first digit and the other for the second digit.

In the NBA and WNBA, you *can* wear the numbers 1 through 9. The great George Mikan, the NBA's first superstar, who played in the 1940s and 1950s, wore 99. Why the difference between the NCAA and the pro leagues? The NBA and WNBA have always allowed any uniform number, and that rule hasn't changed. NBA and WNBA refs usually just call out the number to the scorekeepers, who sit by the side of the court.

# PENCIL ***POWER***

Let's get down to some numbers! Write down these possible uniform numbers on a sheet of paper. Then gather some friends and give them 10 seconds to see if they can circle all the numbers that can't be worn in an NCAA game. Who is the biggest hoop-head in your group?

16

22

37

5

13

9

47

41

1,322

(OK, this one's a trick—the numbers can't be more than two digits.)

61

MARC GASOL REACTS TO SEEING HIS NUMBER CALLED.

**ANSWERS:** 9, 16, 37, 47, 61 (and 1,322!)

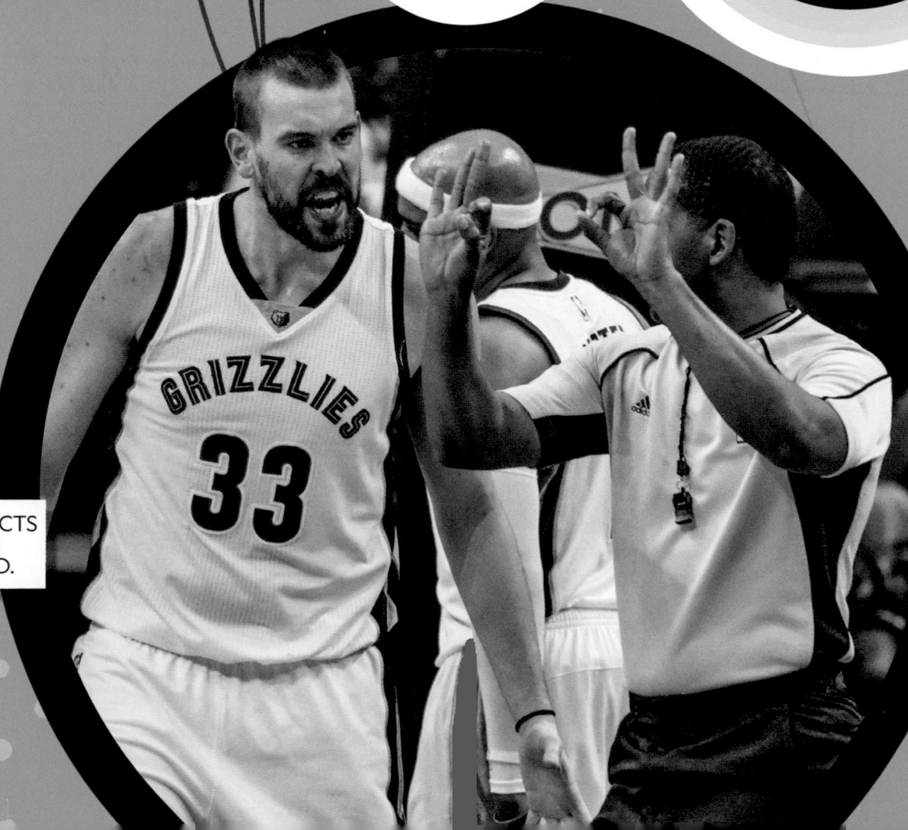

# FAMOUS UNIFORM NUMBERS

**T**o hoops fans, certain jersey numbers say a whole lot. Lovers of the game see some uniform numbers and know exactly who they belong to. Here are some of the most famous uniform numbers around and the players who made them memorable.

## 9

### LISA LESLIE

Leslie once scored 101 points in a high school game; she also led the University of Southern California (USC) to the national championships in college, and she helped the L.A. Sparks win two WNBA titles. To top it off, she won four Olympic gold medals with the U.S. women's basketball team!

## 00

### ROBERT PARISH

He was a very good player for the Celtics and helped them win championships, but he's famous as much for this uniform number as anything else (and yes, we know a double zero is technically not a "number," math fans). Why 00? When Parish played in junior high school, he said there weren't enough numbered jerseys for all the players, so his jersey was called double zero. He kept it.

## 8

### KOBE BRYANT

Kobe Bryant is the only NBA player to have two different jersey numbers retired by the same team. When a team retires a jersey number, it means that another player can't wear that number for that specific team again. Bryant wore numbers 8 and 24 for the Los Angeles Lakers over his 20-year career. He was so good, the Lakers felt they had to retire both!

## 6

### BILL RUSSELL

This epic player won 11 NBA championships, two NCAA titles, and an Olympic gold medal. It's no surprise his jersey number became legendary. (Russell wore No. 6 in college before the NCAA changed the rules about uniform numbers—see page 44.)

## 24

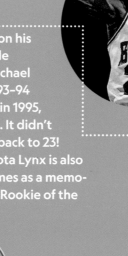

## 23

### MICHAEL JORDAN
### LEBRON JAMES
### MAYA MOORE

LeBron James wears number 23 on his jersey. This was the number made famous by basketball legend Michael Jordan. Jordan retired for the 1993–94 season and decided to come back in 1995, when he wore number 45 for a while. It didn't work for him, and he soon switched back to 23! Maya Moore of the WNBA's Minnesota Lynx is also on her way to joining Jordan and James as a memorable 23; Moore was the 2011 WNBA Rookie of the Year and the 2014 MVP.

## 33

### LARRY BIRD
### KAREEM ABDUL-JABBAR

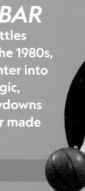

Boston Celtic's Larry Bird had epic battles with Magic Johnson on the court in the 1980s, which brought the NBA front and center into the public eye. Playing alongside Magic, Abdul-Jabbar was part of these showdowns too. Together, Bird and Abdul-Jabbar made 33 a memorable number in the NBA.

## 44

### JERRY WEST

Smooth and steady: West was one of the top guards of the 1960s and 1970s. Over the course of his career, he averaged a terrific 27.0 points per game. He was at his best in the playoffs. Four times, he was tops in playoff scoring.

### MAGIC JOHNSON

The ultimate point guard, and the leader of the Los Angeles Lakers during his time on the team, Johnson (whose real first name is Earvin) was nicknamed "Magic." After his playing career, he showed a little magic, too. Johnson is a very successful businessman and is now part-owner of the Lakers.

## 32

# PLAYERS BY THE NUMBERS

Basketball players, like all athletes, are measured and weighed and counted. Coaches and teams need to know *all* about a player to help figure out their potential. In basketball, one of the most important measurements is height—obviously! Over the years, some players have been much taller or even much shorter than average. From NBA and WNBA records, here are the players who stood out (or up or down) more than others!

## Tallest

**NBA**
**Manute Bol and
Gheorghe Muresan**
7 feet 7 inches (2.3 m)

**WNBA**
**Margo Dydek**
7 feet 2 inches (2.2 m)

## Shortest

**NBA**
**Tyrone "Muggsy" Bogues**
5 feet 3 inches (1.6 m)

**WNBA**
**Shannon Bobbitt**
5 feet 2 inches (1.6 m)

Manute Bol

Gheorghe
Muresan

Margo Dydek

Tyrone "Muggsy"
Bogues

Shannon Bobbitt

**PLACE YOUR HAND HERE**

## Big Hands!

The NBA doesn't keep complete historical records on player hand size, but check out this drawing. How does your hand compare to small forward Kawhi Leonard's 9.75-inch (24.8-cm)-long hand?

9.75-inch (24.8-cm)-long

Kawhi Leonard's Hand Size

# HOW CAN A HUMAN HAVE A WINGSPAN?

Did you know humans have wingspans? Your wingspan is the measurement from the tip of your longest finger on one hand to that of the other hand when your arms are spread wide.

NBA players often have enormous wingspans. One particular player for the New Orleans Pelicans is famous for his uber-wide wingspan. When he was drafted out of the University of Kentucky into the NBA, Anthony Davis stood 6 feet 9¼ inches (2.1 m) tall. His wingspan, however, was a tremendous 7 feet, 5½ inches (2.3 m) long! That's a difference of 8¼ inches (21 cm)! To put that in perspective, the average adult man's arms are about 2 inches (5 cm) longer than his height.

Why is wingspan a big deal in hoops? Well, if two guys are both tall and one can reach farther than the other to make a shot or snag a rebound, that's a major advantage. In fact, scouts and coaches take wingspan into consideration when choosing players.

## DIGIT-YOU-KNOW?

Of all birds, the wandering albatross has the longest wings from tip to tip. So who would win for biggest wingspan in a head-to-head matchup: bird or basketball star? It's the albatross. At 11 feet 6 inches (3.5 m) across, the animal outstretches Anthony Davis by just a bit.

## Pencil Power

Get a measuring tape and gather some friends. Start measuring your wingspans and see who has the longest or shortest. Make a number line and mark your measurements on it. Scientists say that nearly all people's wingspans are usually just a bit longer than their height. How does your wingspan measure?

**ANTHONY DAVIS**

**7 feet 5 ½ inches** (2.3 m)

# TRY *THIS!*

## Put on your striped shirt, pick up your whistle, and loosen up your fingers. It's time to "Be the Ref!" for a big college game.

First, study the chart shown here. See how a ref uses different fingers and hands to show player uniform numbers? After you've become familiar with the hand signals for each number and practiced, it's time to play Be the Ref!

Gather a few friends to start the game. Perhaps you can go head-to-head with one of them. Have one pal say a number between 1 and 99. Remember, since this is a college game, the numbers 6, 7, 8, and 9 aren't allowed. Your friend can throw in some trick numbers that use these digits, but you have to yell out "Trick number!" before saying the number. See how fast you can move your fingers to signal the number called … or how fast you can blow the whistle and shout "Trick number!"

Check out these examples of signals for different numbers.

23

44

51

30

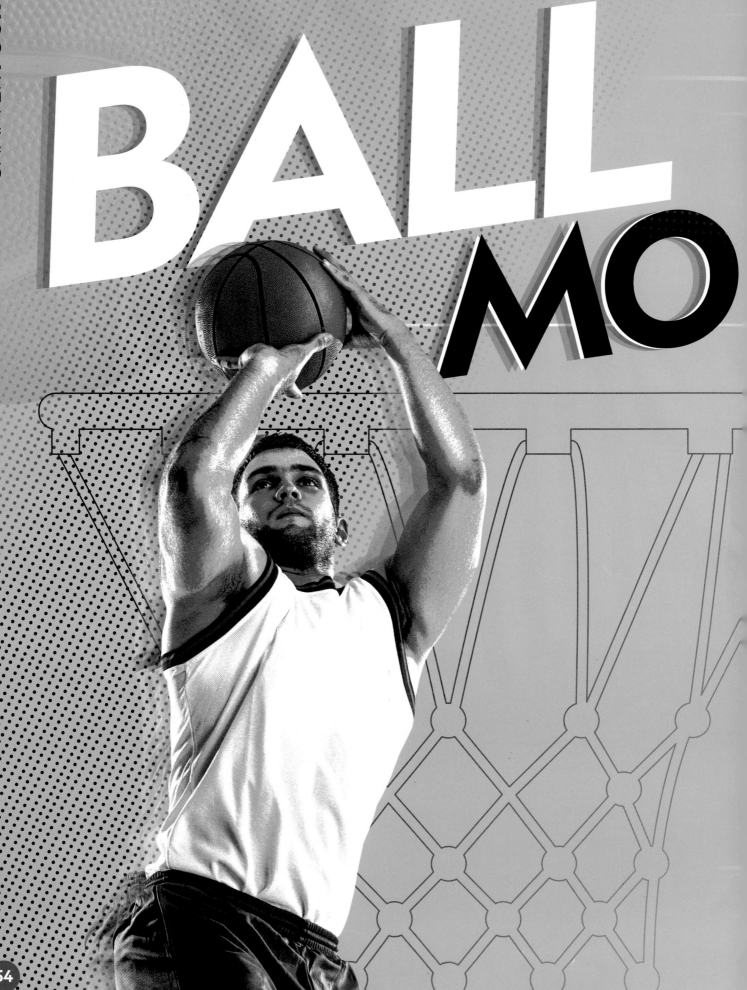

# CHAPTER FOUR

# BALL
# MO

**VEMENT**

**B**asketball is geometry in motion. A round ball moves in a lot of straight and curved lines through space. All these lines and movements create shapes and angles. Along with geometry, basketball is based on the science of physics. Physics explains how and why things move. Understanding the geometry and physics of hoops can make watching (and playing!) the game more fun.

So, get out your calculators, rulers, and protractors, and follow a basketball as it arcs and bounces across the court!

### SCIENCE STUFF

What goes up must come down. When shooting (or making a long pass), basketball players must put enough force on the ball to overcome the force of gravity that is pulling the ball back down. For longer shots or passes, a second force called drag (the resistance created by air moving over an object) has to be overcome. The challenge is to find just the right amount of upward force to send the ball up, toward the basket, and into the hoop!

# DRIBBLING

We're not talking about when a beverage trickles down your chin! Dribbling is how players get the basketball from one spot to another without carrying it. (Walking or running while holding the ball is not OK in basketball.)

Dribbling is a huge part of a team's offense. Players have to be able to keep the ball bouncing as they crisscross the court. Sometimes a dribble is just to get the ball upcourt. Other times a dribble can be used to move around a defender. In chapter five, we'll look at the ball itself; here, we'll talk about what the players do with it.

## When Push Comes to Shove

Dribbling takes force. In the case of dribbling, force is the energy that comes from your hand pushing the ball toward the ground. As the ball bounces back up, you have to give it more force to make it bounce again.

Here are some key tips for a good dribble:

**1** Dribble with your fingertips, not your palms.

**2** Try not to look at the ball as you dribble. Instead, you should be watching out for opponents or searching for a clear path to the basket. It takes practice, but the more you can dribble while looking up, the better you'll play.

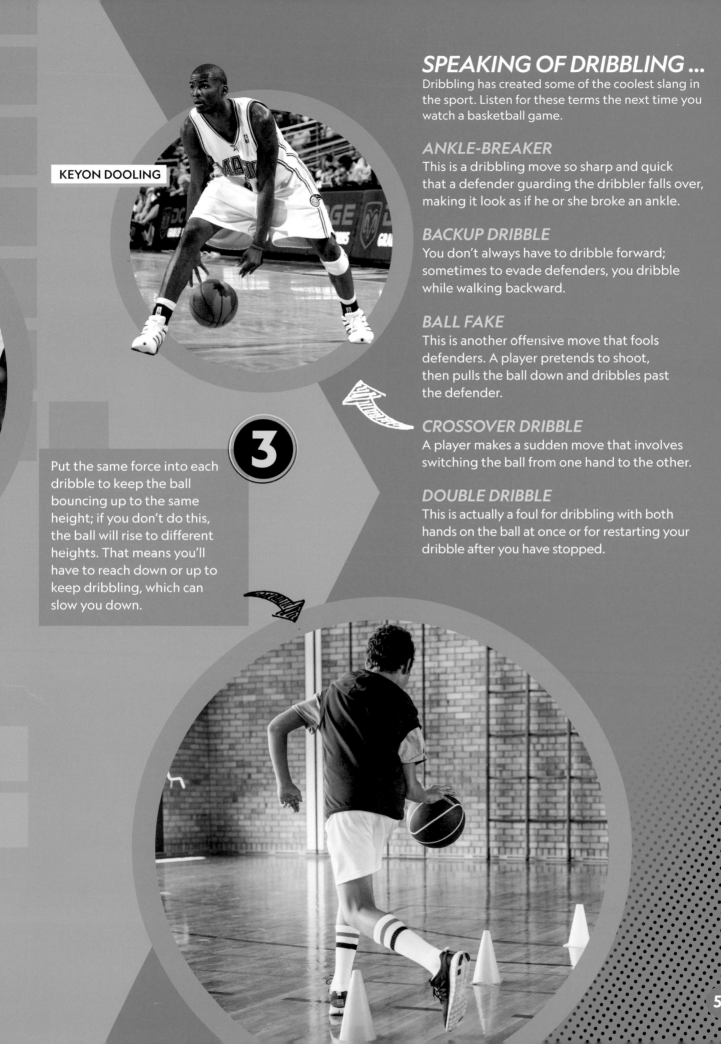

**KEYON DOOLING**

**3**

Put the same force into each dribble to keep the ball bouncing up to the same height; if you don't do this, the ball will rise to different heights. That means you'll have to reach down or up to keep dribbling, which can slow you down.

# SPEAKING OF DRIBBLING ...

Dribbling has created some of the coolest slang in the sport. Listen for these terms the next time you watch a basketball game.

## ANKLE-BREAKER

This is a dribbling move so sharp and quick that a defender guarding the dribbler falls over, making it look as if he or she broke an ankle.

## BACKUP DRIBBLE

You don't always have to dribble forward; sometimes to evade defenders, you dribble while walking backward.

## BALL FAKE

This is another offensive move that fools defenders. A player pretends to shoot, then pulls the ball down and dribbles past the defender.

## CROSSOVER DRIBBLE

A player makes a sudden move that involves switching the ball from one hand to the other.

## DOUBLE DRIBBLE

This is actually a foul for dribbling with both hands on the ball at once or for restarting your dribble after you have stopped.

# LET IT PASS

Passing the ball is a big part of any basketball game. Check out the different types of passes players use and the math and science behind them in the pages ahead.

## BOUNCE PASS

In basketball, bouncing the ball onto the court with both hands to send it to a teammate is an awesome way to pass. The bounce pass is a standard part of every player's skill set. It takes practice, but knowing a little about the geometry of the pass can help: When a ball is bounced onto the court at an angle, it will bounce away from you at about the same angle.

**A GOOD BOUNCE PASS** will end up about waist-high so that a player can easily grab it.

**A BAD BOUNCE PASS** is thrown from too high and so it bounces too high for it to be easily caught.

## STAT STORY

Bounce passes might seem like they're only good for short distances, but that's not always the case. In a 2018 WNBA game, forward Gabby Williams of the Chicago Sky threw a pass from several feet behind the half-court line. It bounced into the path of teammate Allie Quigley about 60 feet (18 m) down the court. The ball went right into Quigley's hands, and she laid it in for an easy bucket.

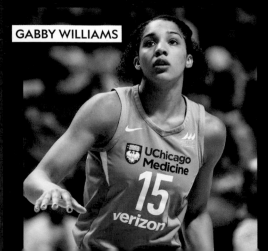

GABBY WILLIAMS

**ANOTHER KEY TO A GOOD BOUNCE PASS** is using the same amount of force in each hand as you throw down the ball. If you push too hard with either hand, the pass will go to the right or the left and not straight ahead.

A BOUNCE PASS IS A GREAT WAY TO MOVE THE BALL TO A TEAMMATE, EVEN IF THE PASSER IS CLOSELY GUARDED.

# CHEST PASS

Remember how using equal force with both hands was key to the bounce pass? It's the same for the chest pass. This is another basketball basic that relies on physics. By throwing a round ball straight out at chest level and using the same force with both hands as you throw, you can send the ball soaring in a straight line.

The best way to do this is to form a diamond with your fingers on the back of the ball, your thumbs at the bottom and your index fingers at the top. Your fingers don't have to touch; in fact, if they're spaced a little, that's better. Then push straight ahead at the target. Snap your wrists to the outside to get more force for longer passes.

CAPPIE PONDEXTER

BETTY LENNOX

# LOB *IT!*

Not all passes bounce or move in straight lines. The lob pass follows more of an arc or a curve. It can get the ball to a teammate across the court. Lobs can be thrown like a chest pass, but they are aimed upward instead of straight ahead. Lobs can also be thrown from overhead like a soccer throw-in. A good lob pass is not too high—that would give the defense time to get to the target. The pass is also not too low—a tall player might just leap up and snag it!

Want to become a lobbing legend? As with other moves, it's all about practice. Keep trying to throw lob passes until you find the right angle and power you need to reach your teammate.

## STAT STORY

### Throwing It Down

The alley-oop is one of the most exciting plays in basketball. A player floats a lob pass near or even at a height above the rim. Another player leaps to meet the ball close to the rim, grabs it, and slams it home. It takes practice for the jump and the pass to meet at the right time. When they do, the crowd goes wild!

DERRICK WILLIAMS

KOBE BRYANT

# THE PERFECT SHOT

**U**sing some geometry and physics know-how, you can make the perfect shot. A basic basketball shot has three parts: setup, shot, and follow-through.

**START WITH THE STANCE:** Your feet, hips, and chest should be square to the basket. Most coaches want the foot on your shooting-hand side to be a little in front of the other foot. This provides you with a little more stability and sets up a platform for the force you will put into the ball when you shoot.

**HOLDING THE BALL:** Your shooting hand goes on the back of the ball, toward the bottom. Your non-shooting hand rests on the side of the ball. Hold the ball like this in front of your chest. Keep your shooting elbow close to your body. Scientists say that holding your shooting arm at about a 52-degree angle from the floor will often result in the best shot (see the Shooting Angles diagram). It's not foolproof, but it's a good start!

**THE SHOT:** Push up and toward the basket with your hand, straightening your elbow as you go up. Snap your wrist at the top to make the ball spin backward as it leaves your hand (see Backspin Rules on page 65). Then watch as the ball soars into the air. The path of a basketball as it travels through the air to the basket is called a parabola. It's basically an arc that is the same shape going up as it is coming down.

**ADD THE LEGS:** With practice, you can do all this while you jump straight up off the ground—the famous jump shot. Energy from your jump transfers into your hand, which transfers into the ball, which sends it flying hoop-ward. The jump shot makes it easier to shoot over other players, and it looks cooler! But the fundamentals are the same: Set your stance, hold the ball, push up, snap the wrist. One study showed that shooting this way (which on average adds one to two feet [30.5 to 61 cm] to the height of the shot) made it up to 17 percent more likely that the ball would go into the basket!

# SCIENCE OF
# *THE SHOT*

The angle at which a player shoots a ball affects the chances of scoring. As you just read, a shot taken at a 52-degree angle is ideal. In fact, one study found that shooting at this angle will result in more clean shots (ones that don't hit the backboard or rim) for nearly all shooters. Now, a player can't exactly pause a game to measure the angle of a potential shot with a protractor. Instead, athletes get plenty of practice.

Even with practice, not every player is going to shoot at exactly 52 degrees. To be a successful swisher, it's also about finding the right angle for you. You just want to be sure to shoot at an angle that allows the ball enough room as it passes through the hoop. This diagram shows how much room there is between the ball and the inside front edge of the hoop when a player shoots. As you can see, there is more room for the 9.4-inch (23.9-cm) ball to go into a standard 18-inch (45.7-cm) rim if you shoot at 45 or more degrees.

## SHOOTING ANGLES
■ 55° angle   ■ 45° angle   ■ 30° angle

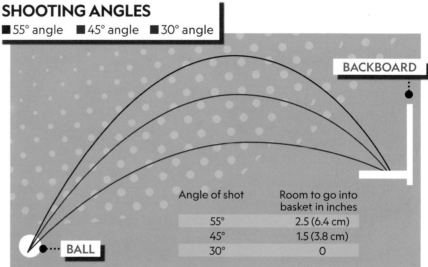

BACKBOARD

BALL

| Angle of shot | Room to go into basket in inches |
|---|---|
| 55° | 2.5 (6.4 cm) |
| 45° | 1.5 (3.8 cm) |
| 30° | 0 |

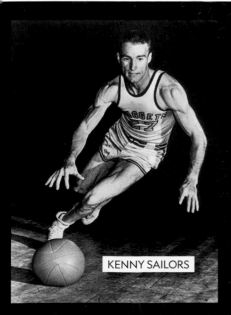

KENNY SAILORS

# STAT STORY

The jump shot is a key way to score in basketball. But the game had been played for more than 40 years before it became a regular move. Early players mostly kept both feet planted on the floor and shot from their chest, pushing the ball toward the net. In 1934, a boy named Kenny Sailors took a leap when making a shot during a one-on-one game with his brother. He was not the first to do it, but he was the first to make it popular. He perfected his jump shot during high school and college, using it to score a ton of points and become a basketball star. In the 1940s and 1950s, the NBA's Jumpin' Joe Fulks impressed fellow players by scoring points using his own version of the jump shot—leaping into the air and twisting left or right before releasing the ball. By the 1960s, jump shots were a permanent part of the game.

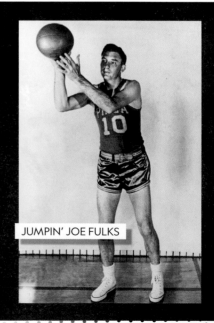

JUMPIN' JOE FULKS

# TAKE IT TO THE BANK

Nothing but net! That's what you hear announcers say when the ball goes directly into the basket without touching the rim or backboard. But a lot of shots can take advantage of the flat backboard, bouncing off it and into the hoop. In fact, some players purposely aim shots to do this. These are called bank shots because the ball banks, or bounces, off the backboard before swishing through the net.

BOGDAN BOGDANOVIĆ

## BACKSPIN RULES

Remember that in shooting a ball you want to give it a backspin. The reason has to do with physics. If a spinning object hits a barrier, it tends to bounce off in the direction of its spin. So, if a ball is spinning backward when it hits the backboard, it will bounce backward—in other words, toward the net.

Try to shoot a bank shot like a chest pass, with no spin. Try to score a bank shot throwing overhand like a baseball. Now flip one up there with backspin. See the difference?

## STRAIGHT OR SIDE?

Bank shots can be taken from anywhere on the court. But most are taken from off to one side of the basket. Shots taken from closer to the front of the basket usually aren't bank shots—for the most part, these don't need to hit the backboard to go in. And in these instances, aiming above the rim to hit the board first is actually a harder shot. That's because if you're in front of the basket, you have to hit the backboard at just the right spot to make the ball bounce into the hoop.

From the side, however, you have a wider "aim point," or target: the backboard instead of just above the rim. The ball will bounce at about the same angle off the backboard as the angle at which it hits the board, hopefully dropping right into the net.

However, there's a point at which you don't have much backboard to aim at and a bank shot won't work too well. It's when you're too far to one side of the basket, say, in the corner of the court. To find out where that point is, see the chart in the Digit-You-Know? box below.

CHUCKY ATKINS, LEFT, AND RODNEY WHITE, RIGHT

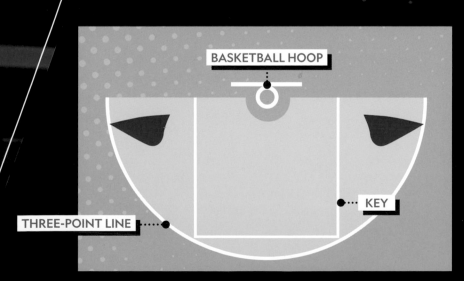
BASKETBALL HOOP
KEY
THREE-POINT LINE

## DIGIT-YOU-KNOW?

Scientists at North Carolina State University programmed a computer to simulate more than a million shots at a basket. After crunching the data, they found spots on the court where a bank shot was 20 percent more effective than a direct shot. Check out this diagram and see if shooting banks from the red areas is better for you, too!

# THE *LOWDOWN* ON **LAYUPS**

According to the laws of physics, objects in motion tend to stay in motion. And a layup is a shot made right near the basket while the player is in motion. So to make a layup, you need to be running or jumping toward the basket. You don't throw the ball at the basket or the backboard as in a regular shot. You use the momentum of your movement toward the basket to give force to the ball, "laying" it on the backboard and into the hoop. That's why it's called a layup and not a throw-up. Well, OK, there's probably more than one reason for that!

Try this experiment to understand the physics of layups. Hold a tennis ball and start jogging. Toss the ball straight up in front of you. Make sure it goes up straight, but keep running. Does the ball fall straight down, with you running past it? Or does it keep going forward and land back in your hand? Spoiler alert: It keeps moving forward. That's also how layups work!

NNEKA OGWUMIKE

# DUNK *STUFF*

Dunking is jumping. And jumping is physics. Players run toward the basket. They use the energy in their legs to push down against the floor. The energy pushes them up off the ground. The more force they can generate from their legs, the higher they can go.

The key is for players to make the top of their jumps—the highest point of their arc-shaped path through the air—be the point at which their arm can reach the basket's rim. That part of dunking just takes training.

And all those spins and twirls and reverse 360s that basketball players do in the lead up to a dunk? It may look like magic, but it comes from training and practice.

## STAT STORY

Lots of stars can do a windmill dunk. Vince Carter, an NBA veteran with more than two decades of experience playing for multiple teams, was one of the most famous. In the windmill dunk, a player like Vince cradles the ball with one hand and wrist. He rotates his arm 360 degrees, making a full circle, like a spinning windmill. The circle is closed when his arm reaches the rim and the ball is slammed through.

**VINCE CARTER**

**ZION WILLIAMSON**

# THE *SCOOP* ON *FREE THROWS*

You've just been fouled and awarded a free throw. You're standing 15 feet (4.6 m) from the basket. No one is guarding you. And you've got 10 seconds, much more than you'd get for a regular shot in a game. Just throw the ball into the basket. How hard can it be, right?

You'd be amazed. One of the easiest shots in the game can be very hard to make. Some of the greatest stars in pro hoops history were terrible free-throw shooters! Wilt Chamberlain (see page 117) was one of the great point-scorers of all time. But he only made about half of his free-throw attempts. The best shooters from the "charity stripe" (a nickname for the free-throw line) can make 90 to 95 percent of their attempts. And some of the greatest free-throw shooters of all time never played in a pro game. They were people who practiced the move over and over in order to set or break world records for sinking the most free throws in a row.

## Taking a Stance

Is there a perfect free-throw form? As you read on page 63, launching the ball at a 52 degree angle reportedly gives you the best chance to make a free throw, but mostly it just takes practice. It's the same shot from the same location every time. So when you find a free-throw form that suits you, keep using it. Your muscles will remember the motion; doing it exactly the same every time is the key to success. Watch the pros—they try to always follow the same free-throw routine. They often even have rituals they repeat before taking the shot—a bounce of the ball, a spin, a practice flick without the ball. Repeating this ritual helps keep them focused.

## DIGIT-YOU-KNOW?

These non-pros could really throw! In 1993, a 71-year-old man named Tom Amberry made 2,750 free throws in a row without missing. It took him 12 hours and made him a legend. Amberry had perfected a form that gave him swish after swish. In 1996, Ted St. Martin topped Amberry, making 5,221 free throws in a row. Bob Fisher (right) goes for speed: He once made 2,371 free throws in an hour (though he missed a few in that time). That's one every 1.5 seconds!

TIFFANY MITCHELL
OF THE USA
NATIONAL TEAM

## STAT STORY

Nearly all pros and top college players shoot free throws the same way: overhand. Some, however, use an underhand form that can be very effective. Rick Barry was the most famous NBA star to use it, and he led his league in free-throw percentage seven times! (Free-throw percentage is the number of successful free-throw shots out of the total number of attempts made.) Underhanders spin the ball backward as they let go with both hands from below their waist (see Backspin Rules on page 65 for details). The launch angle is steeper, which makes the angle at which the ball enters the hoop steep as well. A steeper angle generally means that there is more room around the ball as it goes through the rim, allowing it to swish right through the basket. Give it a go, it might work for you, too!

# TRY *THIS!*

You've read how players pass and shoot—now it's your turn!

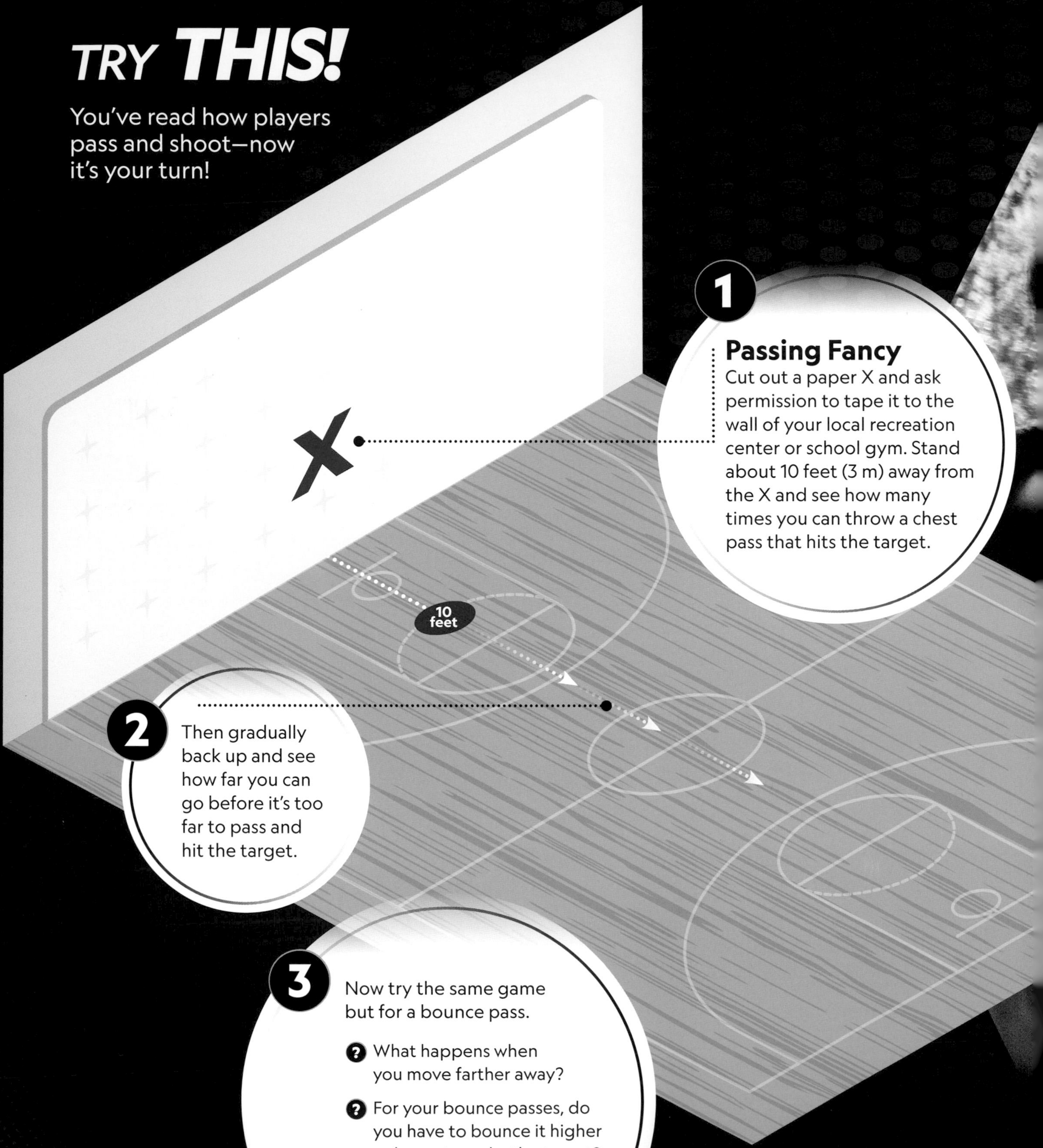

**1**

## Passing Fancy
Cut out a paper X and ask permission to tape it to the wall of your local recreation center or school gym. Stand about 10 feet (3 m) away from the X and see how many times you can throw a chest pass that hits the target.

X

**10 feet**

**2** Then gradually back up and see how far you can go before it's too far to pass and hit the target.

**3** Now try the same game but for a bounce pass.

**?** What happens when you move farther away?

**?** For your bounce passes, do you have to bounce it higher or lower to make the target?

**?** What's your record?

**?** Can you improve with practice?

## Free-Throw Contest!

Get your friends together and see who is the best free-throw shooter. Make sure to take turns practicing first. Then see who can make the most in a row without a miss. Try it a bunch of times. With all that practice, did your streaks get longer? To add a twist, use a timer to see who can make the most free throws in 30 seconds (someone will have to rebound for the shooter).

## *FOR EXTRA-BONUS FUN*

See who can make a free throw blindfolded! A man named Stuart Robbins broke the world record for this neat trick, making 16 baskets in a row with his eyes covered!

# CHAPTER FIVE

# IT'S ALL ABOUT THE

# GEAR

**B**asketball looks like a sport with pretty simple gear—just a bouncing ball, a pair of sneakers, and a metal hoop. How complicated can that be? You'd be surprised! Let's get the ball rolling and look at the numbers and science behind basketball equipment.

## DIGIT-YOU-KNOW?

Painted on NBA and WNBA backboards is a rectangle that is 24 inches (61 cm) across and 18 inches (45.7 cm) tall. Why? It's there to give shooters a target. Most gyms have see-through plastic backboards. Without the tape, it would be hard to get a good "read" on distance needed for a shot. The tape is also a target for some bank shots; hit a corner of the square and the ball will bounce into the hoop!

# GET A GRIP

Take a close look at a basketball. You'll see little bumps all over the outside of the ball. It's thanks to these bumps—called pebbles—that you can grab, pass, shoot, and grip the ball. Without them, the ball might often slip out of your hands. What's the story behind the bumps? James Naismith tried using slick soccer balls when he first founded the sport, but the ball kept slipping out of players' hands. In 1894, Naismith met with Albert G. Spalding, a former baseball star turned sporting goods developer and salesperson. Yes, *that* Spalding, whose name is on every NBA ball. After Naismith asked him to create the first basketball, Spalding came up with the idea of making the leather on a basketball's surface rougher with little pebbly dots. Each pebble acts as a point of contact when the ball meets another surface, like your palms and fingertips. More points of contact between two surfaces causes more friction, a force that resists motion. This allows for a better grip. Naismith and Spalding's pebble design was so effective that it hasn't been changed in more than a century.

**1 INCH
(2.5 CM)**

**1 INCH
(2.5 CM)**

**122 PEBBLES**

## HOW MANY PEBBLES ARE ON A BASKETBALL?

OK, this is your homework: Pick up a basketball and count all the pebbles. Ready? Go! Just kidding. That would take way too long and may hurt your eyes. There are about 122 pebbles per square inch (19 per sq cm) of leather on a high-quality indoor basketball. The entire surface area of the ball is about 286 square inches (1,845 sq cm). So to get the total number of pebbles, multiply 122 by 286 and you get 34,892. Leaving room for a few extra here and there, the total number of pebbles is about 35,000.

**NBA BALL**

## STAT STORY

### Trouble on the Road

When U.S. basketball pros play in other countries, they have to use a different ball. And it's harder for them to handle! The Japanese-made Molten brand—the official ball used by FIBA—is slicker on the outside, say the pros. The main difference has to do with the shape and texture of the little pebbles on the Molten ball. These pebbles are not as round or soft as those on a Spalding. FIBA balls also have 12 panels, more than the NBA's eight. The circumference (or the distance around the ball) is 30.7 inches (78 cm). The NBA ball is a tiny bit smaller at 29.5 inches (74.9 cm) around. Though these measurement differences are small, together they make a difference.

**MOLTEN BRAND FIBA BALL**

CARMELO ANTHONY (LEFT) OF THE USA AND KONSTANTINOS TSARTSARIS (RIGHT) OF GREECE SCRAMBLE FOR THE BALL IN A 2008 OLYMPIC BASKETBALL GAME.

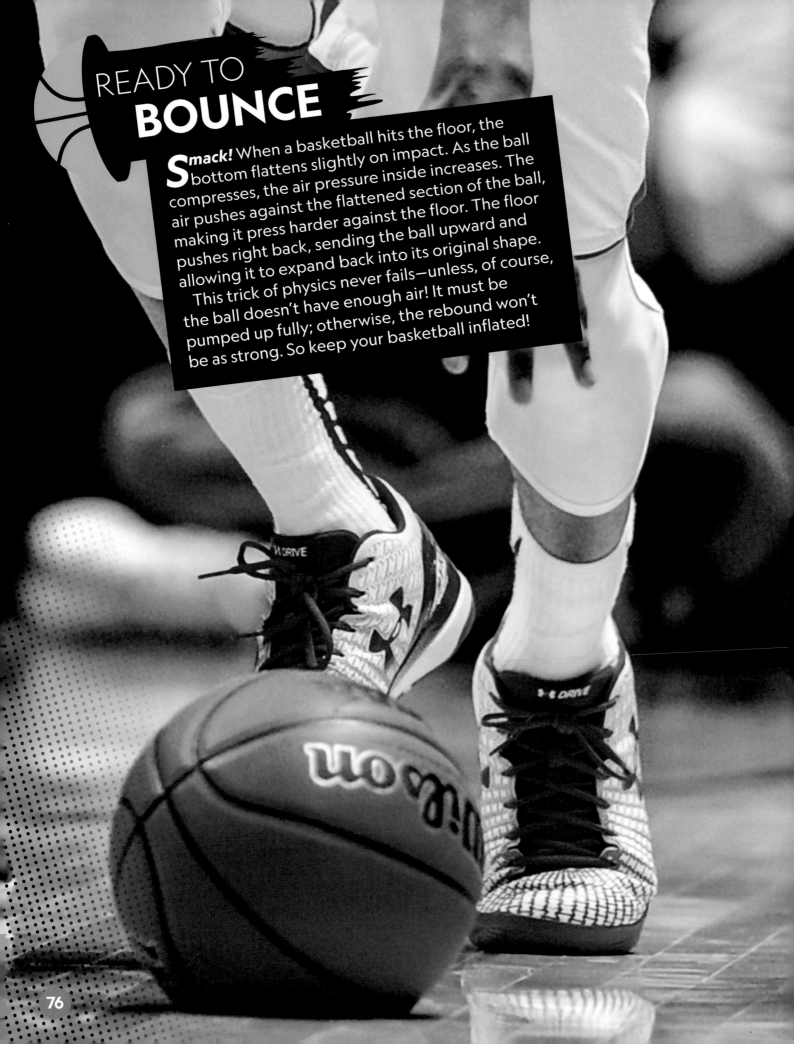

# READY TO
# BOUNCE

**Smack!** When a basketball hits the floor, the bottom flattens slightly on impact. As the ball compresses, the air pressure inside increases. The air pushes against the flattened section of the ball, making it press harder against the floor. The floor pushes right back, sending the ball upward and allowing it to expand back into its original shape. This trick of physics never fails—unless, of course, the ball doesn't have enough air! It must be pumped up fully; otherwise, the rebound won't be as strong. So keep your basketball inflated!

## Leather vs. Rubber

Most of the basketballs you have in gym class or in your garage are probably made of rubber. They bounce well on just about any surface. But in the pros and top college and high school games, the ball is leather on the outside. That leather shell surrounds a rubber bladder that is filled with air. Is leather better? Players say the leather gives them a better grip. Rubber balls tend to bounce a bit higher too, which makes them harder to control. But leather basketballs are for indoors only; asphalt or concrete courts will ruin them.

VINTAGE LEATHER
BASKETBALL

## *SCIENCE STUFF*
### *Dribble Details*

When you dribble a basketball, why doesn't it just keep bouncing even without your help? It has to do with gravity and the transfer of energy. Gravity pulls the ball down. And as the ball falls and hits the ground, it loses some energy. Part of its energy changes to sound (*boing!*). Some of its energy goes into changing the shape of the ball (from round to briefly flat where it hits the floor). To make it bounce to the same height again, you have to put that energy *back into* the ball by propelling it with your hand. So don't start your dribble until you're ready. The ball won't dribble itself.

# AT THE *RIM!*

A 7-foot-2-inch (2.2-m) giant in a jersey rushes toward the basketball hoop, leaps into the air, and smashes down a dunk so hard that the rim breaks off and the glass backboard shatters. The crowd goes wild! Well, that was cool to watch, but also dangerous and expensive.

More than one basketball player has demolished the basket during an energetic dunk. Luckily, science had a solution to keep this from happening. A man named Arthur Ehrat invented a device to protect the glass and the players. He created a powerful spring to connect the back of a basket's rim to the backboard that lets the rim bend down when pulled on. The spring didn't affect how a ball bounced into the hoop, but it could handle the weight of a player. Once the player let go, the rim sprung back into place. This spring became a standard part of NBA games in 1981. In 2009, the league switched to a flexible rim that bent on the front and at the sides.

DARRYL DAWKINS SHATTERS THE BACKBOARD IN 1979.

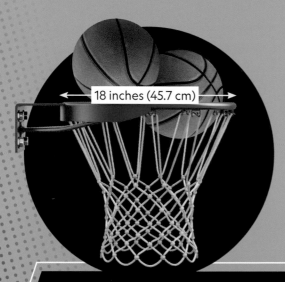

18 inches (45.7 cm)

ALEX LEN SHOWS HOW THE SPRING-LOADED RIM BENDS.

## DIGIT-YOU-KNOW?

How big is a basketball hoop? Well, it's larger than a basketball, right? In fact, it's almost twice as wide. An NBA ball has a diameter (the distance across at the middle) of 9.4 inches (23.9 cm). A hoop is 18 inches (45.7 cm) across. That means you could almost fit two balls in it side by side.

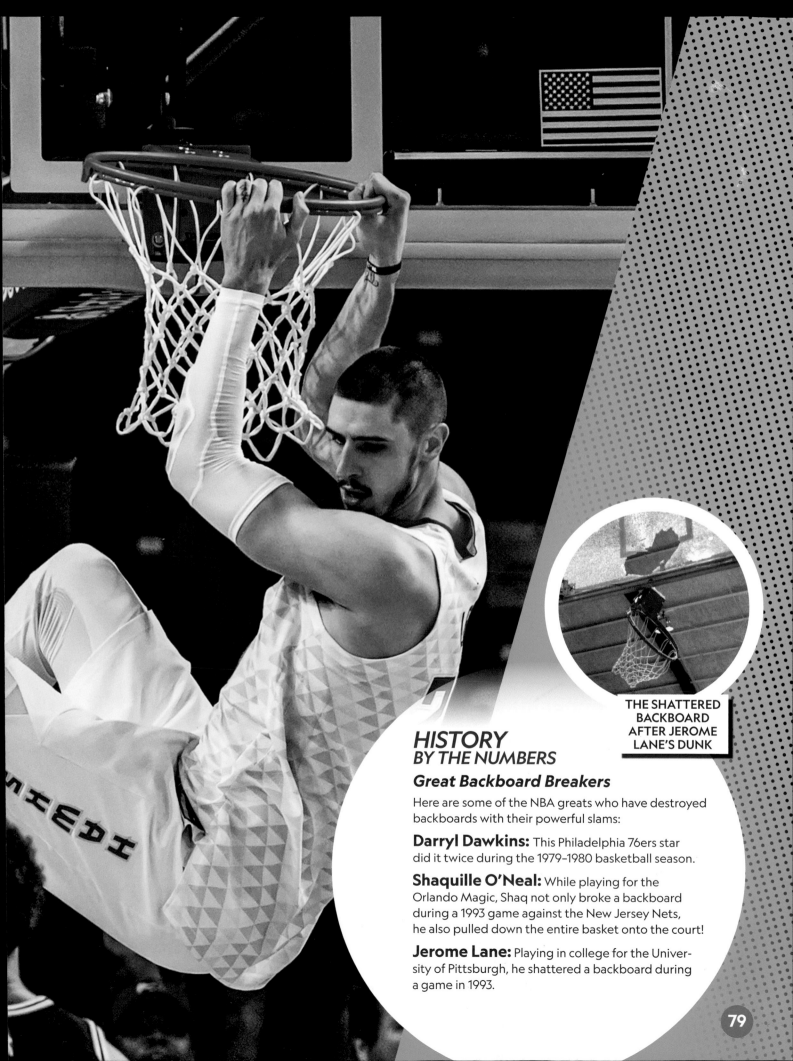

THE SHATTERED BACKBOARD AFTER JEROME LANE'S DUNK

## HISTORY
### BY THE NUMBERS

#### Great Backboard Breakers

Here are some of the NBA greats who have destroyed backboards with their powerful slams:

**Darryl Dawkins:** This Philadelphia 76ers star did it twice during the 1979–1980 basketball season.

**Shaquille O'Neal:** While playing for the Orlando Magic, Shaq not only broke a backboard during a 1993 game against the New Jersey Nets, he also pulled down the entire basket onto the court!

**Jerome Lane:** Playing in college for the University of Pittsburgh, he shattered a backboard during a game in 1993.

# SNEAKER TECH

In basketball, having the right pair of sneakers can be the key to success. Basketball shoes have come a long way over the course of hoops history. In the mid-20th century, players were all about the canvas Chuck Taylor shoe line made by Converse (see Stat Story below). Air Jordans, originally created by Nike for Michael Jordan, became a hit with consumers in the 1980s.

Since then, shoemakers have explored just about every kind of tech you can imagine to come up with awesome new kicks for players. Companies today use synthetic materials, high-tech rubber, and special lightweight fabrics to produce shoes. They can even custom-make sneakers to fit just one person's feet.

When it comes to basketball shoes, must-have features include lightness, traction, ankle support, and cushioning. Let's take a closer look.

**1** *LIGHTNESS:* It's hard enough to jump high without heavy shoes weighing you down. When looking for the best basketball shoes, players look for the perfect combination of support and strength, with lightweight materials that don't bring them down, like nylon and polyester.

**2** *TRACTION:* The rubber bottoms of basketball shoes need to grip the wood floors as a player makes a sharp cut, or quick change of direction. Slick shoes would cause players to slip and slide on the court.

## STAT STORY

### *Who Was Chuck Taylor?*

The Converse Chuck Taylor sneaker was the classic NBA shoe for most of the 1950s and 1960s. Plain white, high-topped, and made of canvas, it was pretty plain compared to today's electrifying shoes. Chuck Taylors were named for a former basketball player who was a pro in the early 1900s and later worked for Converse. Taylor knew what basketball shoes should do and helped Converse design the famous sneakers. To thank him, Converse put his name on the footwear. Chuck Taylors may not be the number one shoe used by basketball players today, but they're still pretty popular: As of 2015, the company reported selling 270,000 pairs of "Chucks" a day!

## IF THE SHOE FITS

So, you're on the hunt for some new basket-ball shoes. Don't just buy the coolest-looking pair. Make sure they fit well! Have your feet professionally measured at an athletic-shoe store. If you're primarily looking for speed, choose a flexible shoe with a moderate cushion. If you're a power player, you'll want an extra-stable shoe with maximum cushioning. Sneaker experts suggest doing a few B-ball moves in the store to test their comfort factor. Jump, spin, and pivot in the shoes. Check that the shoes aren't too tight. You should be able to slip a finger between the back of the shoe and your ankle.

**ANKLE SUPPORT:** Many pros wear high-tops of some sort. Because they lace up around the ankles, these shoes can add stability, helping to keep ankles from twisting during sharp cuts.

**3**

**CUSHIONING:** What goes up must come down. When players land, they want their shoes to help soften the impact on their feet, which a well-cushioned shoe can help with.

**4**

## DIGIT-YOU-KNOW?

NBA players often get a new pair of shoes after only a couple of games. The Denver Nuggets' equipment manager said that some hoopsters swap out their shoes after every game and every practice. That adds up to more than 100 pairs of sneakers per player each season!

# SHORTS
## *GO LONG!*

Try these NBA numbers on for size. The shorts worn by early pro players were pretty short. The length from the waistband to the bottom of each leg was only about eight or nine inches (20.3 or 22.9 cm). By the 1970s, these measurements had extended by four or five inches (10.1 or 12.7 cm). Then came Michael Jordan. He wore his shorts a bit longer than everyone else. And what Jordan did, everyone wanted to do, so shorts got longer. By the early 2000s, some "shorts" were more than 24 inches (61 cm) long—that's past the players' knees!

In recent seasons, shorts have shrunk, just a bit. We will probably never again see shorts as small as those worn in the olden days of basketball, but the full-on Jordan baggies are going to be rare, too.

RANDY SMITH, 1973

| 1930 | 1940 | 1950 | 1960 | 1970 |

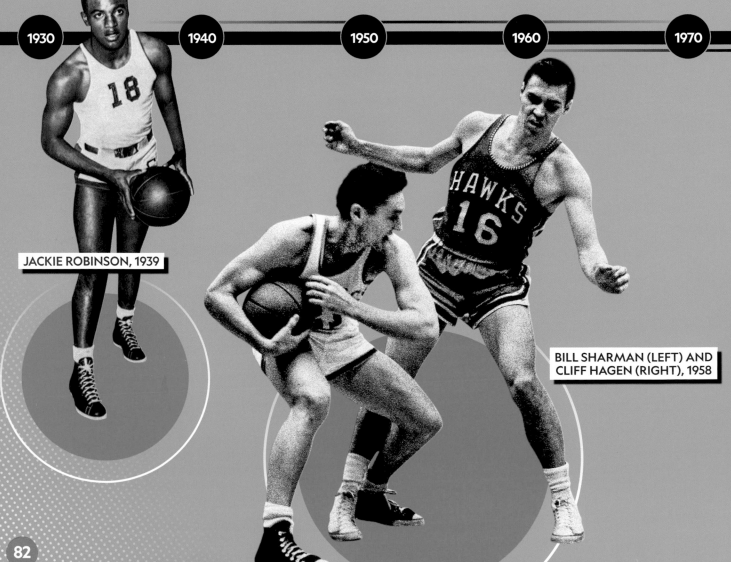

JACKIE ROBINSON, 1939

BILL SHARMAN (LEFT) AND
CLIFF HAGEN (RIGHT), 1958

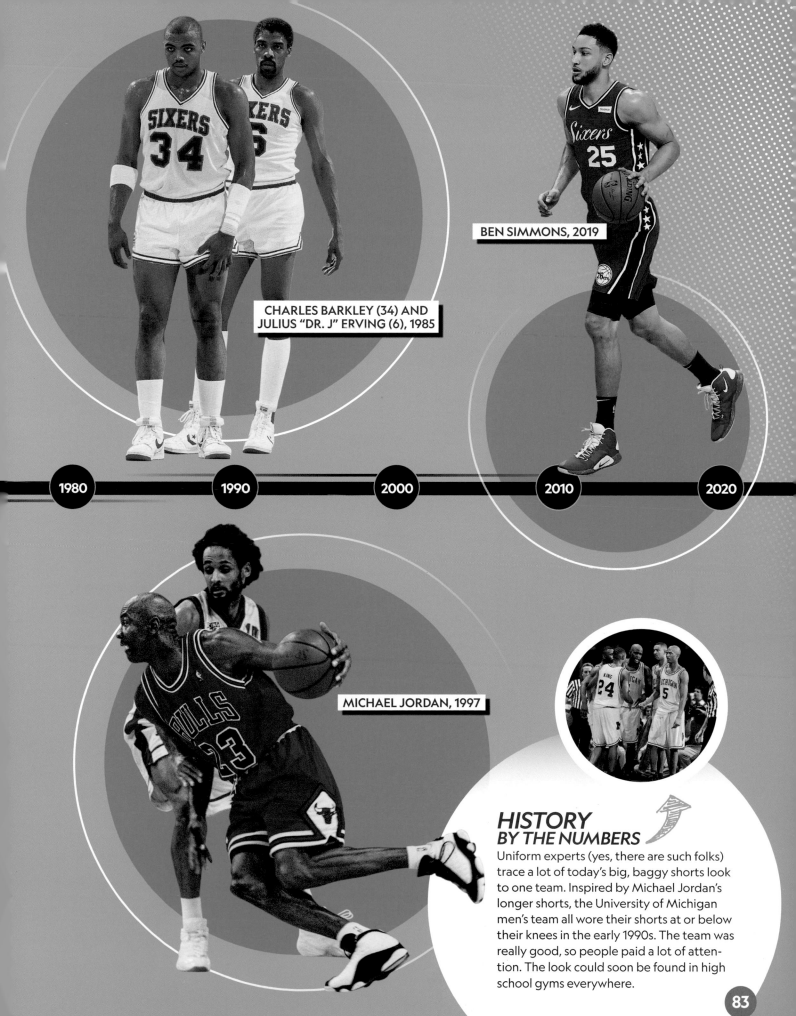

CHARLES BARKLEY (34) AND
JULIUS "DR. J" ERVING (6), 1985

BEN SIMMONS, 2019

1980  1990  2000  2010  2020

MICHAEL JORDAN, 1997

## HISTORY
### BY THE NUMBERS

Uniform experts (yes, there are such folks) trace a lot of today's big, baggy shorts look to one team. Inspired by Michael Jordan's longer shorts, the University of Michigan men's team all wore their shorts at or below their knees in the early 1990s. The team was really good, so people paid a lot of attention. The look could soon be found in high school gyms everywhere.

# TRY **THIS!**

Tap into your inner designer. Ask an adult to help you find blank basketball shoe and uniform templates online, or draw your own, like the example shown here. Then see if you can come up with a revolutionary new design that will amaze the basketball players you know.

## TIPS

Head to the shoe store for inspiration. What are the hot colors? What patterns and designs are used? Will your new shoe be for a particular team? What about your company logo?

# TIPS

Check out NBA uniforms. Many teams now have several alternate jerseys that they wear. The Golden State Warriors have even experimented with short sleeves instead of tank tops. Find a new way of letting fans know what a player's name and number are— be creative!

# TIPS

Research lightweight materials and even new high-tech fabrics. Is there something you can make your uniforms from that will help players move better or stay warm or cool, depending on where they're playing?

# CHAPTER SIX

# STAT

| Point FG | | 3-Point FG | | Free Throw | | Rebo... | | ...overs | Fouls | Total Points |
|---|---|---|---|---|---|---|---|---|---|---|
| ...t. | Made | Att. | Made | Att. | Made | O... | | | | |

**TWO POINTS!**

**HIT A THREE!**

**SIX-FOR-EIGHT FROM THE FIELD!**

**FT PCT! APG!**

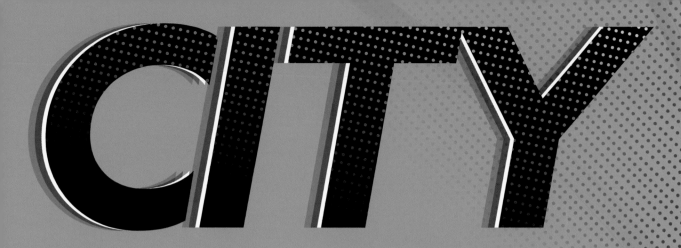

**CITY**

*B*asketball athletes are supertalented, and it's fun to watch them show off their skills. But to really dive into hoops, you need to know the stats. How do teams, players, and fans keep track of who did what? What are the key statistics to know? What are the statistics of the future?

Being tall, fast, athletic, and hardworking can help a basketball player become a superstar. Understanding basketball math and numbers can help *you* become the ultimate hoops fan!

### HISTORY BY THE NUMBERS
Though computers and tablets are essential for tracking stats in today's pro and college basketball scene, some scorekeepers still start with an old-school No. 2 pencil. They keep track of information on paper charts like this one and then transfer the answers into computer programs and spreadsheets.

# COUNT 'EM UP

The most important number in a basketball game is the score. Points are added up as the game goes on. When the buzzer sounds, the team with the most points wins. That's not exactly breaking news!

But numbers fill a hoops game from tip-off to final shot. In every game, scorekeepers, fans, fantasy players (more on that later), coaches, scouts, and, yes, the players, are tracking numbers of all sorts. Here are the key "counting stats" in basketball.

***Try to answer the trivia question that goes with each stat!***

Answers are at the right side of page 89.

## Rebounds

When a shot misses the basket and bounces back into the court to a player, it's called a rebound. Either team can snag a rebound ball. Offensive players can quickly try another shot. Defensive players start the action toward their own basket.

**?**

**Which of these is a real nickname for rebounding: wiping up, cleaning the glass, or picking cherries?**

## Points

You get these, of course, when the ball goes into the basket. Field goals are two points, free throws are one point. Baskets made from outside the three-point line are, naturally, worth three points.

**When can you get two points without the ball going in the basket?**

## Assists

Basketball is a team game. Players don't score without help (usually). If a player makes a pass that leads directly to a basket, he or she gets an assist. These stats are one of the hardest to track since the game moves so fast.

**The name of what U.S. coin is also the nickname for an assist?**

## Steals

In basketball, stealing is legal. In fact, it is encouraged! Quick-handed players can swat the ball from an opponent (without hitting their body, of course). It doesn't happen that often, but when it does, it can change a game quickly.

**In real life, stealing is a crime. What criminal phrase is sometimes heard on a basketball court after a steal?**

## Blocked Shots

Taller players can often smack down an opponent's shot as it soars upward on its path to the basket. (They're not allowed to do this when the ball is traveling downward.) These are called either blocks or blocked shots.

**The opposite of a block is when a player dunks over a taller player trying to block. What's the slang term for when that happens in a spectacular fashion?**

## Turnovers

A steal is when an opposing team member nabs your ball. It is a kind of turnover—when you "turn over" the ball to the other team. Other types of turnovers occur when a pass is intercepted or a player dribbles the ball out of bounds. When that happens, the other team then gets the ball. No one likes turnovers except the opponent!

**In basketball, is the ball in or out of bounds if it bounces on the sideline or end line?**

**TRIVIA ANSWERS Points:** If a player knocks away the ball when it is on the rim or when the shot is moving down toward the basket, that is a foul called goaltending. The referee awards the shooter's team two points (or three, if it is a three-point shot). **Rebounds:** Cleaning the glass. **Assists:** A dime. **Steals:** "That defender just picked his pocket!" **Blocked Shots:** If you get dunked on while trying to block, you just got "posterized." (Why "posterized"? Because when this action goes down, it looks like something that should appear on a poster!) **Turnovers:** It's out of bounds. Compare that to soccer, for example, in which the whole ball has to be outside the line to be out.

# COUNT 'EM UP ...
# ALL SEASON LONG

As each season moves along, the numbers come pouring in and keep adding up. What players had the best seasons? For the answers, you gotta look at the stats! On these pages, we look at single-season records for players in the NBA, WNBA, men's NCAA, and women's NCAA. FYI: NBA teams play 82 games a season, whereas WNBA seasons are 34 games long. NCAA Division 1 men's and women's teams play more than 30 games per season, depending on how far they go in the playoffs.

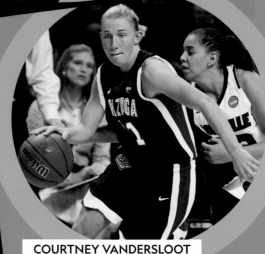

**COURTNEY VANDERSLOOT**

| LEAGUE | NBA | WNBA | NCAA M DIVISION 1 | NCAA W DIVISION 1 |
|---|---|---|---|---|
| **POINTS** | **4,029** Wilt Chamberlain 1961–62 Philadelphia Warriors | **860** Diana Taurasi 2006 Phoenix Mercury | **1,381** Pete Maravich 1969–1970 Louisiana State University | **1,109** Kelsey Plum 2016–2017 University of Washington |
| **ASSISTS** | **1,164** John Stockton 1990–91 Utah Jazz | **258** Courtney Vandersloot 2018 Chicago Sky | **406** Mark Wade 1986–1987 University of Nevada, Las Vegas | **367** Courtney Vandersloot 2010–2011 Gonzaga University |
| **REBOUNDS** | **2,149** Wilt Chamberlain 1960–61 Philadelphia Warriors | **404** Sylvia Fowles 2018 Minnesota Lynx | **734** Walt Dukes 1952–1953 Seton Hall University | **539** Courtney Paris 2005–2006 University of Oklahoma |
| **STEALS** | **301** Alvin Robertson 1985–86 San Antonio Spurs | **100** Teresa Weatherspoon 1998 New York Liberty | **160** Desmond Cambridge 2001–2002 Alabama A&M University | **192** Chastadie Barrs 2018–2019 Lamar University |
| **BLOCKED SHOTS** | **456** Mark Eaton 1984–85 Utah Jazz | **129** Brittney Griner 2014 Phoenix Mercury | **207** David Robinson 1985–1986 U.S. Naval Academy | **223** Brittney Griner 2009–2010 Baylor University |
| **TURNOVERS** | **464** James Harden 2016–17 Houston Rockets | **135** Ticha Penicheiro 1999 Sacramento Monarchs | **167** Trae Young 2017–2018 University of Oklahoma | Not recorded |

# GOING UP AND DOWN

This bar graph shows the total points made by the single-season points leader during the first NBA season of each decade from the 1950s on, plus the 2018–19 season. Even though players have gotten bigger and stronger over the years, the number of points scored has not always gone up each decade.

## Single-season record for points scored

| Season | | |
|---|---|---|
| 1950–51* | George Mikan | 1,932 |
| 1960–61 | Wilt Chamberlain | 3,303 |
| 1970–71 | Kareem Abdul Jabbar | 2,596 |
| 1980–81 | Adrian Dantly | 2,452 |
| 1990–91 | Michael Jordan | 2,580 |
| 2000–01 | Jerry Stackhouse | 2,380 |
| 2010–11 | Kevin Durant | 2,161 |
| 2018–19 | James Harden | 2,818 |

*NBA teams played only 68 games during the 1951–52 season.

WILT CHAMBERLAIN

JERRY STACKHOUSE

# SUPER STATS

Stats stack up over the long careers of top players. For the all-time records in key NBA stat categories, check out page 123. There, you'll see the familiar names of legendary NBA superstars. However, there are other all-time stat kings and queens who you might not know about. Meet some players who made a big mark in the NBA and WNBA record books.

## NO. 99

When he retired in 1954, George Mikan was the NBA's leader in career points, with 10,156. That may not be as high as what many later players did, but without Mikan, basketball would not be nearly as popular as it is today. Mikan was the league's first big star. His skills around the basket put the NBA on the sports map. He led the league in scoring in its first three seasons and led in rebounds during one season. He was famous not only for his hook shot (a shot made while standing sideways to the hoop by moving the ball in an arc with the far hand), but also for being one of the only players to wear eyeglasses and the number 99 on his jersey.

## LADY MAGIC

Nancy Lieberman didn't just break records, she broke barriers. In 1976, she was the youngest Olympic basketball medalist ever at 18. She then led her Old Dominion University team to three national titles, while setting a school record for assists. She later became the first woman to play in a men's league, the U.S. Basketball League. When the WNBA began in 1997, she played, even though she was 39—that's years past the average age of retirement for most pro athletes! She was later a coach in the WNBA. In 2018, she became the first woman to lead a men's team to a title—as head coach of the Power in the BIG3 League, she led her team to the BIG3 championship.

# THE DOCTOR *IS IN*

Julius "Dr. J" Erving led the ABA in scoring for three different seasons and scored more than 30,000 points between his ABA (1971–76) and NBA (1976–87) careers. But what he was most famous for were his soaring, swooping, gravity-defying dunks. The Doc turned the game into an acrobatics show. There are dunks he made that no one has been able to match yet!

# INTERNATIONAL *STARS*

Dirk Nowitzki starred for the Dallas Mavericks from 1998 to 2019. He scored more than 31,000 points and led the Mavs to an NBA Championship title. Born and raised in Germany, Nowitzki is the all-time NBA leader in points by a player born outside the United States. Steve Nash is third all-time in assists with 10,335. The Canadian, who played for multiple NBA teams, is the top out-of-towner in that category.

# MR. *THREE*

As of the 2018–19 season, Ray Allen was atop the NBA all-time list, with 2,973 three-point baskets made. He led the NBA in scoring three-point shots for three seasons and had 10 seasons with 150 or more treys, or three-pointers. More than any other player before Stephen Curry, Allen put the three-pointer on the NBA map.

# WNBA *ROYALTY*

Bow down to Lisa Leslie. She may have retired in 2009, but she is still sixth all-time scorer in WNBA history, with 6,263 points, and third in rebounds, with a total of 3,307. No other player can match that versatility. She was a seven-time All-Star, helped the L.A. Sparks win two championship titles, and also won four Olympic gold medals for the United States.

# THE ABCS OF PPG

In the 2018–2019 season, LeBron James scored 2,251 points to James Harden's 2,191. But Harden was the NBA scoring champion for that season. How is that possible?

Here's the deal: Instead of yearly totals, the NBA uses per-game averages to determine the scoring leader. James played in 82 games, whereas Harden was only in 72, due to an injury. In part because he played in more games, James had more points overall. But Harden had an average of 30.4 points per game (ppg), beating out James, who averaged 27.5. How do the scorekeepers get these numbers?

Time for a calculator! They take the total number of points a player scored during a season and divide by the number of games played. The result is the average number of points a player scored in each of his or her games. That is how the NBA figures out its scoring champ. The same is true for all of the counting stats, from rebounds to blocks. It's what you average *per game* that really counts, not the total score for the season.

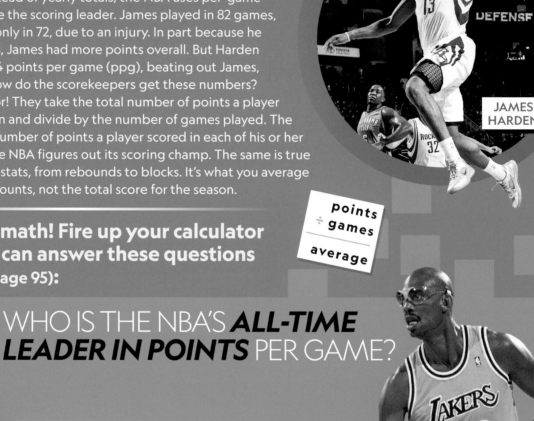

JAMES HARDEN

points ÷ games
—————
average

**Let's do some math! Fire up your calculator and see if you can answer these questions** (answers are on page 95):

## WHO IS THE NBA'S *ALL-TIME LEADER IN POINTS* PER GAME?

**MICHAEL JORDAN**
**32,292** points in **1,072** games

**or**

**KAREEM ABDUL-JABBAR**
**38,387** points in **1,560** games

# WHO HAD THE *MOST CAREER ASSISTS* PER GAME?

**JOHN STOCKTON**
**15,806** assists in **1,504** games

**or**

**MAGIC JOHNSON**
**10,141** assists in **906** games

# WHO HAD THE *HIGHEST BLOCKS-PER-GAME AVERAGE* IN NBA HISTORY?

**HAKEEM "THE DREAM" OLAJUWON**
**3,830** blocks in **1,238** games

**or**

**MARK EATON**
**3,064** blocks in **875** games

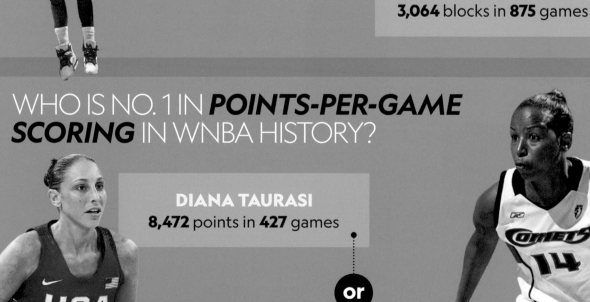

# WHO IS NO. 1 IN *POINTS-PER-GAME SCORING* IN WNBA HISTORY?

**DIANA TAURASI**
**8,472** points in **427** games

**or**

**CYNTHIA COOPER**
**2,601** points in **124** games

**ANSWERS:** Jordan: 30.12 ppg; Johnson: 11.19 apg; Eaton: 3.50 bpg; Cooper: 20.98 ppg

# PERCENTAGE PARTICULARS

Another way to track stats is by using percentages. A percentage is a number that can reveal how often something happens. For example, if you take 10 shots and 5 of them go in, you made 50 percent of your shots. To get this number, you divide the portion of shots that were made by the whole number of attempts. So, 5 divided by 10 equals 0.5. Multiply that number by 100 and, ta-da, you get 50 percent.

More math? Yes, please! Let's see how you do in figuring out these NBA single-season records. We did the first one for you as the tip-off. Check your answers on the bottom right side of page 97.

## BEST THREE-POINT SHOOTING PERCENTAGE (THE PERCENTAGE OF MADE SHOTS) AMONG ACTIVE NBA PLAYERS, AS OF 2018

$$2{,}129 \div 4{,}880$$
$$0.436$$
$$0.436 \times 100$$
**43.6%**

NBA
STEPHEN CURRY
**4,880** attempts, **2,129** made

## BEST SHOOTING PERCENTAGE, SINGLE SEASON

NBA
WILT CHAMBERLAIN, 1972–73
**586** attempts, **426** made

WNBA
TAMIKA RAYMOND, 2003
**193** attempts, **129** made

## STAT STORY

Shaquille O'Neal was a superstar, clearly one of basketball's best ever players. He was a dominant force on the glass and could score a ton of points. But he had one downfall: He wasn't so good as a free-throw shooter. "The Diesel" tried everything, but he could never master this shot. He averaged only 52.7 percent on free throws and never did better than 62 percent in any one season.

# STAT STORY

The all-time best free-throw shooter was Steve Nash. The longtime guard made 90.4 out of every 100 free throws he shot. DeAndre Jordan is excellent at making field goals, sinking 67.3 percent of his shots as of 2018. A big reason for his success is that most of Jordan's shots are from very close to the basket. It's harder to miss a dunk than a shot from 30 feet (9.1 m) away!

STEVE NASH

DEANDRE JORDAN

## BEST FREE-THROW PERCENTAGE, SINGLE SEASON

### NBA
JOSE CALDERON, 2008–09
**154** attempts, **151** made

### WNBA
BECKY HAMMON, 2014
**35** attempts, **35** made

## BEST THREE-POINT PERCENTAGE, SINGLE SEASON

### NBA
KYLE KORVER, 2009–10
**110** attempts, **59** made

### WNBA
TEMEKA JOHNSON, 2012
**64** attempts, **34** made

ANSWERS (BY PERCENTAGE): Chamberlain: 72.6; Raymond: 66.8; Calderon: 98; Hammon: 100; Korver: 53.6; Johnson: 53.1

# TEAM RECORD NUMBERS

It's not just players; teams stack up the stats and numbers, too. Here are some of the coolest team records.

## MOST POINTS BY A TEAM IN A SINGLE SEASON

**10,371**

NBA
DENVER NUGGETS, 1981–82

**3,192**

WNBA
PHOENIX MERCURY, 2010

DAN ISSEL

STEVE JOHNSON

## STAT STORY

### Points Aren't Everything

The Denver Nuggets have the record for most points in an NBA season (1981–82). That's nice, but what they didn't get in that same season was the championship. A big reason they didn't win the league title: While they scored a lot of points, they also gave up a lot of points! They scored a record total of 10,371 points, but they *gave up* 10,328 points. Their final record—46 wins and 36 losses—was good, but they lost in the first round of the playoffs. The WNBA's Phoenix Mercury lost more games than it won in 2010, while scoring a record number of points. So, players: Don't forget to play defense!

# MOST THREE-POINT SHOTS MADE IN A SINGLE SEASON

**1,323**

NBA
HOUSTON ROCKETS, 2018–19

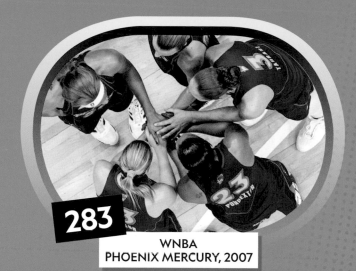

**283**

WNBA
PHOENIX MERCURY, 2007

## MOST WINS, ALL-TIME

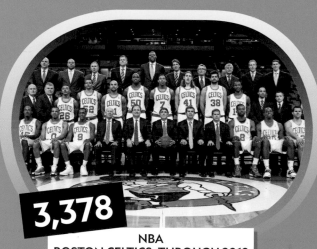

**3,378**

NBA
BOSTON CELTICS, THROUGH 2019

**443**

WNBA
LOS ANGELES SPARKS, THROUGH 2018

## MOST LOSSES, ALL-TIME

**3,053**

NBA
SACRAMENTO KINGS, THROUGH 2019

**425**

WNBA
LAS VEGAS ACES, THROUGH 2018

# PLAYOFF NUMBERS

When the playoffs start, it doesn't matter how much your team scored during the season—the numbers reset to zero. Some players thrive under the pressure of these games, and their stats skyrocket. Here are some of the most memorable numbers in NBA and WNBA playoff history.

## Jordan Overshadows the Suns

Michael Jordan was the king of NBA scoring. He often saved his best for the NBA Finals. Against the Phoenix Suns in 1993 (right), Jordan averaged 41 points per game—the highest scoring average for one championship series. That means that he often scored more than that. He scored 55 points in Game 4 and never scored less than 31 in the six-game series. Wow!

## Curry Crushes

New NBA Finals records are often set every season. In Game 2 of 2018's NBA Finals, the amazing Stephen Curry poured in a record-breaking nine three-point shots. His Golden State Warriors won the game over the Cleveland Cavaliers on the way to their second straight NBA title.

## Fierce Fowles

Sylvia Fowles is one of the toughest players in WNBA history. Her Minnesota Lynx team needed a win in the 2017 WNBA Finals. She came through in a big way, grabbing a WNBA Finals–record 20 rebounds. She scored 17 points too, and the Lynx won the game and the championship!

# STAT STORY

The annual men's and women's NCAA tournaments also pile up numbers. Read more about them on page 106, but here's a preview, with some stats from NCAA tournament history:

**❶ MOST CAREER POINTS, MEN:**
407, **Christian Laettner,** Duke, 1988–1992

**❷ MOST CAREER POINTS, WOMEN:**
479, **Chamique Holdsclaw,** Tennessee, 1995–1999

**❸ MOST POINTS, SINGLE TOURNAMENT, MEN:**
184, **Glen Rice,** Michigan, 1989

**❹ MOST POINTS, SINGLE TOURNAMENT, WOMEN:**
177, **Sheryl Swoopes,** Texas Tech, 1993

**❺ MOST POINTS, SINGLE TOURNAMENT GAME, MEN:**
61, **Austin Carr,** Notre Dame, 1970

**❻ MOST POINTS, SINGLE TOURNAMENT GAME, WOMEN:**
50, **Lorri Bauman,** Drake, 1982

# NEW STATS

As a way to find new ways to win and new ways to choose the right players for a team, the NBA, like other sports leagues, uses math stats and data in many different ways. It's not enough to know how many points a player makes in a game anymore. Number crunchers on every team can now look at a huge variety of different measurements. Here are a few examples of more recent math formulas that have changed the way basketball numbers are crunched.

## True Shooting Percentage (TS%)

On page 96, you looked at the shooting percentages for individual types of shots. Created in the early 2000s, true shooting percentage shows how often a player makes all types of shots combined—field goals, three-pointers, and free throws. The formula is as follows:

Total points divided by twice the field goal attempts (FGA), plus free-throw attempts (FTA) times 0.44. That figure is multiplied by 100 to get the true shooting percentage (TS%).

Here is an example, using WNBA player Liz Cambage's per game averages for the 2018 season.

**Total points: 1443    FGA: 923    FTA: 517    TS% = Total Points/[2(FGA + (0.44 × FTA))] x 100**

| 0.44 |  | (FGA) 923 |  | 1,150.48 |  | 1443 |  | (TOTAL POINTS) 0.627 |
|---|---|---|---|---|---|---|---|---|
| ✕ (FTA) 517 |  | ➕ 227.48 |  | ✕ 2 |  | ➗ 2300.96 |  | ✕ 100 |
| 227.48 |  | 1,150.48 |  | 2,300.96 |  | 0.627 |  | **62.7%** TS% |

## Offensive Rating

This rating uses a variety of stats to figure out how a player impacts his or her team's offensive performance. It looks at how many points are scored for every 100 times the player is in possession of the ball. Elena Delle Donne is the career leader here for the WNBA, with an offensive rating of 123.99. In the NBA, sharp-passing guard Chris Paul is atop the all-time list. His teams average 122.89 points for every 100 possessions.

CHRIS PAUL

ELENA DELLE DONNE

# Player Efficiency Rating (PER)

Measuring all of a player's stats against those of other players can get complicated. Enter PER. The idea of this stat, invented by sportswriter John Hollinger, is to come up with one number rating for each player that can easily be compared to other player ratings. To generate this number, PER uses a formula that takes into account points, assists, offensive and defensive rebounds, time in the game, and even blocks for each basketball player. The formula uses a point value system—that is, it assigns a certain amount of points to each of these actions. It adds together points for a player's positive actions (like assists and free throws) and subtracts points for negative actions (like missed shots and fouls). The resulting stat is then adjusted to figure out how the player performs on a minute-by-minute basis. Not surprisingly, Michael Jordan is the all-time NBA leader, with a 27.91 PER, followed by LeBron James at 27.68. Two-time WNBA MVP Cynthia Cooper, now retired, is that league's number one, at 28.72. The Washington Mystics' Elena Delle Donne is the active leader at 28.19.

MICHAEL JORDAN

## MORE ON STATS

There are numerous cool stats that are calculated in the game of basketball. Here are a few more types and what they measure.

**Win Shares:** How many wins a player contributes to a team through the player's efforts on the court

**VORP (Value Over Replacement Player):** How many points a player is worth over an average player in his or her position

**Pace Factor:** How many possessions of the ball a team has in a game

# HOT SHOOTERS!

Today, some basketball stats are adding up to more than just numbers—they're now being translated into visuals that players can use to improve their game. A great example of this is the heat (or heat zone) map.

Information about thousands of shots is entered into a computer. The data are based on the location of shooting attempts and their success rate. The computer uses the information to produce a color-coded map of the court that shows the success of the various shooting positions, with red representing the spots where a player is most successful (in other words, where the player is a "hot shooter"!) and blue representing where a player is least successful.

## Heat Zone Maps

These heat zone maps show the most and least successful areas of the court where two different players have made shots. Find the places where the shooter being measured is really good and where the player is "colder." You can see that a lot of shots are taken on or close to the three-point line.

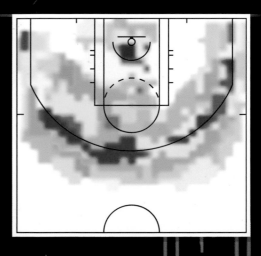

## *SCIENCE STUFF*

Technology is becoming a bigger player in basketball. Some teams and colleges (and even players, using their own apps) are now using shot-tracking technology. Sensors can go in shoes, basketballs, and in the rafters of the arena to track every movement the players make and note when and where shots are taken. The data are gathered into statistical and visual presentations that can be studied by coaches and players to continually improve skill and the game.

# BRACKET MANIA!

Each March and April, the men's and women's NCAA hoops tournament attracts the attention of millions of people. Every Division 1 team has a shot at making the tournament. In the end, only 68 make it to the men's and 64 to the women's. An opening round on the men's side pits the eight lowest-ranked teams against each other, and four teams are eliminated. Then it's on. The remaining 64 teams are divided into four regions, each with 16 teams. The women's teams are divvied up in the same way. They play a furious knockout tournament at sites around the country, all leading up to the Final Four competition between the winners from each region.

Fans cheer for their teams, hoping for a big win. Many—including lots of non-fans—also test their powers of prediction by filling out brackets. A bracket is a diagram that represents a series of games played in a tournament. Fans make guesses about which team will win in each matchup. They have some help: Every team in the tournament is given a "seed," or rank by a committee of experts. In each of the four regions, there are seeds numbered 1 through 16. No. 1 seeds are the very best. No. 16s are just happy to be there. But you don't want to just pick the highest-rated teams for your bracket. During the tournaments, lower-ranked teams can pull off upsets that completely change the game!

**NOTRE DAME VS. CONNECTICUT IN THE WOMEN'S FINAL FOUR NCAA COLLEGE BASKETBALL SEMIFINAL GAME, 2019**

1
16
8
9
5
12
4
13
6
11
3
14
7
10
2
15

1
16
8
9
5
12
4
13
6
11
3
14
7
10
2
15

**THE HARVARD WOMEN'S BASKETBALL TEAM CELEBRATES THEIR WIN OVER STANFORD.**

## PLANTING SEEDS

In all of NCAA tournament history, men and women, only two 16th-seed teams have beaten a 1 seed. In 1988, No. 16 Harvard women's team beat No. 1 Stanford (it's worth mentioning that both of Stanford's stars were injured and couldn't play). The only men's 16 over 1 came in 2018 when the University of Maryland, Baltimore County Retrievers shocked No. 1 Virginia.

**THE UMBC RETRIEVERS CELEBRATE THEIR WIN OVER THE VIRGINIA CAVALIERS.**

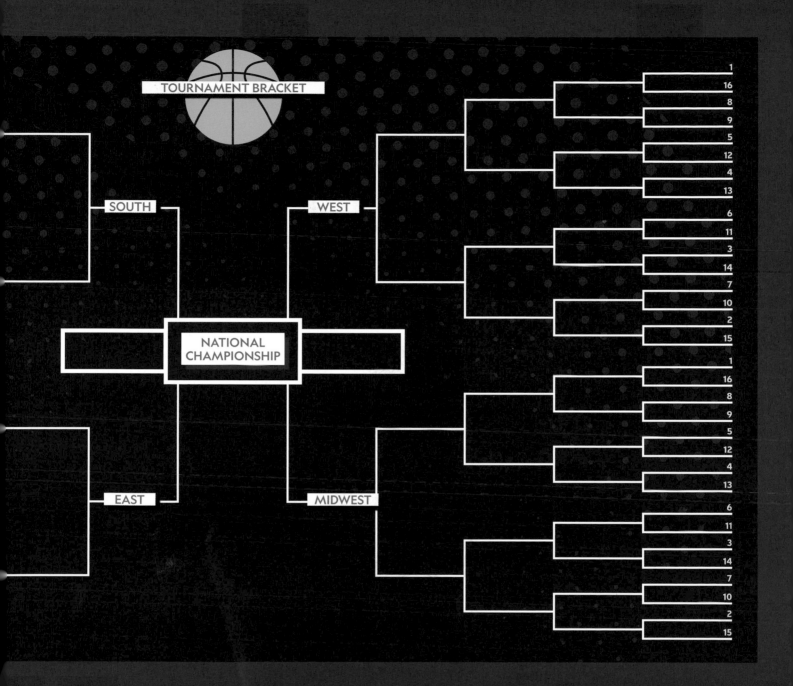

TOURNAMENT BRACKET

SOUTH

WEST

NATIONAL CHAMPIONSHIP

EAST

MIDWEST

1
16
8
9
5
12
4
13
6
11
3
14
7
10
2
15
1
16
8
9
5
12
4
13
6
11
3
14
7
10
2
15

## DIGIT-YOU-KNOW?

In 2019, more than 17.2 million NCAA men's brackets were filled out on ESPN.com alone. Guess how many of those brackets got every game right? Zero! In fact, after the first day, the number of brackets that had just those games correct was only .25 percent! One math professor calculated the odds of correctly predicting every one of the games in the men's NCAA tournament at about 2.4 trillion to one. However, the NCAA did a study that came up with 9.2 quintillion to one. Yikes!

# TRY *THIS!*

## Make Your Own Heat Zone Maps

Find the locations on the court where you're a hot shooter.

## What you will need:

- graph paper
- colored markers
- chalk or tape
- an indoor or outdoor basketball half-court
- a basketball
- several friends to make it interesting

**1 3**

## Steps:

**1** Set up 8–10 marks using chalk or tape on the court at different distances and different angles from the basket.

**2** Draw a map of the half-court on the graph paper and mark the spots you labeled on the court with a box.

**3** Take 10 shots from each of the locations and note on your graph how many out of 10 you made for each.

**4** Use the math skills you learned on page 96 to figure out your shooting percentage at each spot.

**5** Assign colors to each percentage group from 0–20, 21–40, 41–60, 61–80, and 81–100.

**6** After you have all the shots taken and the information recorded, color the boxes at each of the 10 spots on your court map. That's your heat map. You'll see immediately which spots on the court are your "best shots" and which spots you need to work on!

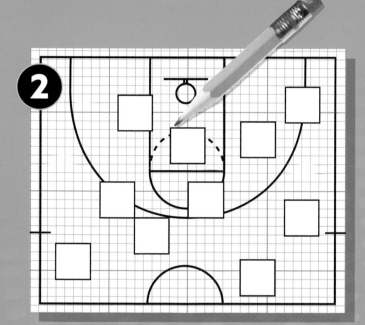

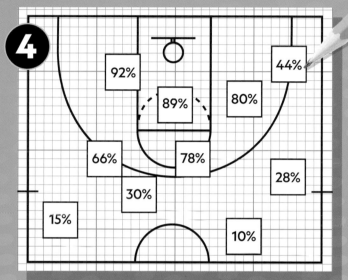

**5**
- 0–20
- 21–40
- 41–60
- 61–80
- 81–100

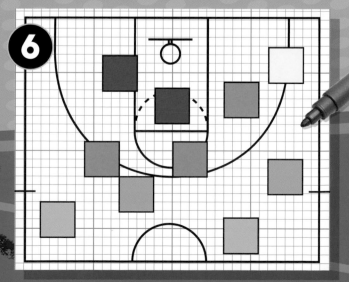

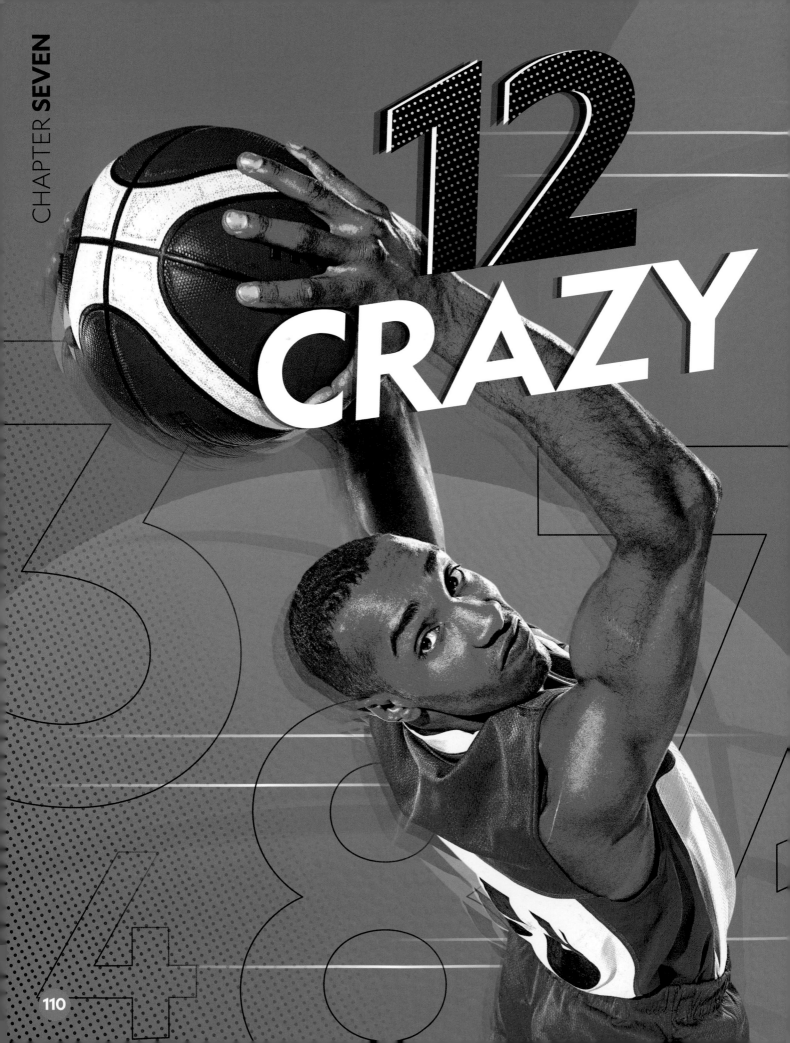

# CHAPTER SEVEN

12

CRAZY

# NUMBERS

**Y**ou've been hit with a swarm of stats, an avalanche of digits, a pile of points, assists, rebounds, and more. In this final section, we look at some of the most famous and important numbers in hoops history, along with cool stories and facts behind the figures. If you really want to call yourself a basketball superfan, these are the numbers to know. So, lace up your sneakers and read on!

## PENCIL POWER

Here's a way for you and your friends to add to your hoops fun. Next time you watch a basketball game together, provide each of your pals with a pencil and a piece of paper listing numbers 1 through 25. Then see how fast each of you can hear or see all these digits in the game. For example, if you see No. 7 on a uniform, check that off the list. If you hear the announcer say that a player is "10 for 13" check off those numbers. Whoever can check off all 25 numerals first is the winner. Switch it up by just counting numbers you see, not the ones you hear. It's game time!

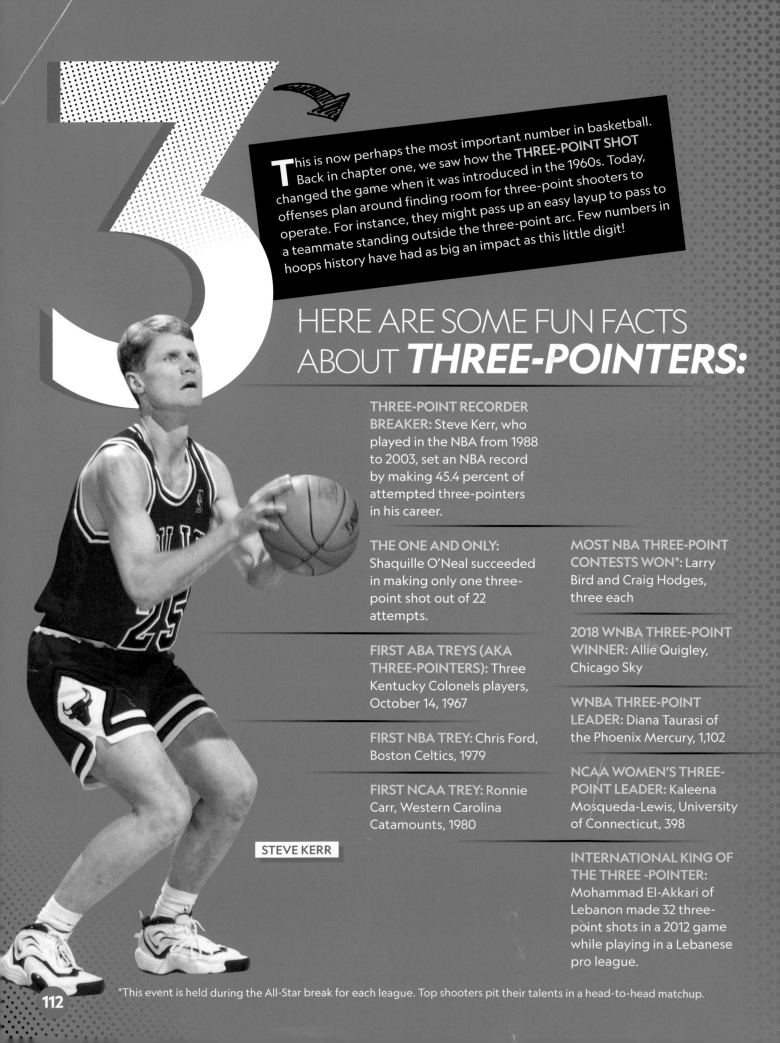

# 3

**T**his is now perhaps the most important number in basketball. Back in chapter one, we saw how the **THREE-POINT SHOT** changed the game when it was introduced in the 1960s. Today, offenses plan around finding room for three-point shooters to operate. For instance, they might pass up an easy layup to pass to a teammate standing outside the three-point arc. Few numbers in hoops history have had as big an impact as this little digit!

## HERE ARE SOME FUN FACTS ABOUT *THREE-POINTERS:*

**THREE-POINT RECORDER BREAKER:** Steve Kerr, who played in the NBA from 1988 to 2003, set an NBA record by making 45.4 percent of attempted three-pointers in his career.

**THE ONE AND ONLY:** Shaquille O'Neal succeeded in making only one three-point shot out of 22 attempts.

**FIRST ABA TREYS (AKA THREE-POINTERS):** Three Kentucky Colonels players, October 14, 1967

**FIRST NBA TREY:** Chris Ford, Boston Celtics, 1979

**FIRST NCAA TREY:** Ronnie Carr, Western Carolina Catamounts, 1980

**MOST NBA THREE-POINT CONTESTS WON\*:** Larry Bird and Craig Hodges, three each

**2018 WNBA THREE-POINT WINNER:** Allie Quigley, Chicago Sky

**WNBA THREE-POINT LEADER:** Diana Taurasi of the Phoenix Mercury, 1,102

**NCAA WOMEN'S THREE-POINT LEADER:** Kaleena Mosqueda-Lewis, University of Connecticut, 398

**INTERNATIONAL KING OF THE THREE-POINTER:** Mohammad El-Akkari of Lebanon made 32 three-point shots in a 2012 game while playing in a Lebanese pro league.

STEVE KERR

*This event is held during the All-Star break for each league. Top shooters pit their talents in a head-to-head matchup.

# 8

The Golden State Warriors (nicknamed the Dubs) received a lot of praise for winning two NBA championship titles in a row in 2017 and 2018. That's pretty impressive, but the championship record goes to the Boys in Green (as the Celtics are called). **THE TEAM EARNED A RECORD-SETTING EIGHT CHAMPIONSHIP TITLES IN A ROW IN THE MID-20TH CENTURY.**

The Celtics were the NBA champs in all of the following seasons:

| | |
|---|---|
| 1958–59 | 1959–60 |
| 1960–61 | 1961–62 |
| 1962–63 | 1963–64 |
| 1964–65 | 1965–66 |

But wait, there's more: The team also won in the 1956–57 season, the 1967–68 season, and the 1968–69 season. That means the Celtics scored a total of 11 titles in a span of 13 seasons.

## STAT STORY

### Biggest Winner

Bill Russell was literally at the center of the Celtics' eight-year winning streak. Russell, who played center for the team from 1956 to 1969, was perhaps the best defensive big man in NBA history. He holds the NBA record for most championship rings, having won 11. For the final two of these, he was the player-coach. (Yep, "Russ" was the team's head coach while still a player. That has been done only a few times in NBA history.) Russell was also the first African-American head coach in U.S. major league sports.

# 11

What's the men's college basketball equivalent to the Celtics? It has to be the University of California, Los Angeles (UCLA). The UCLA Bruins dominated college hoops at about the same time as the Celts were running the pro teams into the ground. Led by legendary coach John Wooden, the Bruins were NCAA champs 10 times in 12 years from 1964 to 1975. **THE BRUINS ADDED ANOTHER WIN IN 1995, GIVING THEM 11 SHINY GOLD CHAMPIONSHIP TROPHIES.**

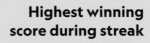

## BRUINS STREAK NOTES

**Average margin of victory**
(Margin of victory is the difference in points between the winning team and the losing team.)

**23.5 POINTS**

**Highest winning score during streak**

**119 POINTS**

**Lowest winning score during streak**

**51 POINTS**

From January 1971 to January 1974, the Bruins won 88 games in a row! That's almost three seasons without losing a game. The streak began with a win over UC Santa Barbara. It was stopped by Notre Dame. UCLA topped the previous record of 60 consecutive wins, which belonged to the San Francisco Dons, by 28 games.

## DIGIT-YOU-KNOW?

These schools have come close to matching UCLA's title total, but they're not quite there yet.

University of Kentucky Wildcats: 8
University of North Carolina Tar Heels: 6
Duke University Blue Devils: 5

# 33

In the NBA, the longest winning streak was set by one of the league's most famous teams. The **LOS ANGELES LAKERS WON 33 GAMES STRAIGHT** between November 5, 1971, and January 9, 1972. They beat the old NBA record set by the Milwaukee Bucks by 13 games. This string of victories was greater than the longest winning streaks in Major League Baseball (MLB), the National Football League (NFL), and the National Hockey League (NHL). Highlights of the streak included a 154–132 win over the Philadelphia 76ers, a 125–120 win over the Houston Rockets (the closest game), and one overtime triumph over the Phoenix Suns. The closest the record-setting Golden State Warriors (see page 118) came to the Lakers' mark was a 28-game streak in 2015. Keep trying, Dubs!

## The Starting Five for 33

These players were the most frequent starters during the Lakers' amazing run:
Wilt Chamberlain (center)
Jim McMillian (forward)
Happy Hairston (forward)
Jerry West (guard)
Gail Goodrich (guard)

## HISTORY BY THE NUMBERS

The NBA logo is a silhouette of a dribbling basketball player and was modeled after a picture of Lakers streak-setter Jerry West. West played point guard and shooting guard for the team from 1960–1974. The logo was created in 1969, and it's how West got his nickname, "The Logo."

115

# 42

**RUSSELL WESTBROOK**

**W**hat do you call it when a player in a game reaches a total number of 10 or more in three stat categories, such as assists, steals, and rebounds? A triple-double! Get it? The triple refers to the three categories and the double refers to the double-digit stat the player achieved in each. It's a difficult NBA feat, calling for a player to excel in several areas. Great shooters don't usually have a lot of assists. Great passers are not usually rebounding aces. Getting a triple-double means you're an all-around awesome hoopster.

In the 2016–2017 season, Oklahoma City Thunder guard Russell Westbrook started racking up triple-doubles at an amazing rate. He got to the final game of the season with 41, tying the NBA record. In that game, he got 10 assists ... 16 rebounds ... and buried a buzzer-beating three-point shot to reach a total of 50 points! TRIPLE-DOUBLE! WESTBROOK'S 42 TRIPLE-DOUBLES FOR THE SEASON WERE THE MOST IN NBA HISTORY.

Perhaps even more amazing was that Westbrook averaged a triple-double for the whole season (see chart)! That had only been done once before by Oscar Robertson, who played for the Cincinnati Royals (see Stat Story). Westbrook topped Robertson by averaging a triple-double again in 2018 and 2019!

## Westbrook's Two Super Seasons

| YEAR | POINTS PER GAME | ASSISTS PER GAME | REBOUNDS PER GAME |
|------|-----------------|------------------|-------------------|
| 2016–17 | 31.6 ppg | 10.4 apg | 10.7 rpg |
| 2017–18 | 25.4 ppg | 10.3 apg | 10.1 rpg |
| 2018–19 | 22.9 ppg | 10.7 apg | 11.1 rpg |

## STAT STORY

### The Big O

The great Cincinnati Royals guard Oscar "The Big O" Robertson was the first NBA player to start accumulating double-digit stats in three categories. At the time—the early 1960s—the feat wasn't yet known as a triple-double. Still, Robertson wowed the crowd with per-game averages of 30.8 points, 11.4 assists, and 12.5 rebounds in 1961–62. The term was coined in the 1980s.

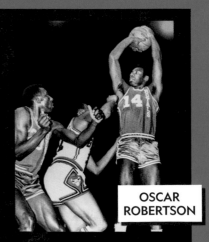

**OSCAR ROBERTSON**

If you were a scorekeeper for the 1961–1962 Philadelphia Warriors, your hands would have gotten pretty tired. Back then, scorekeepers just used pencils and paper, scribbling down new totals whenever a player scored. And, given the way Warriors center Wilt Chamberlain played, they probably went through a *lot* of pencils!

**BILL RUSSELL (LEFT) AND WILT CHAMBERLAIN (RIGHT)**

# 50.4

Wilt the Stilt, as the 7-foot-1-inch (2.2-m) center was called, poured in points at a level never seen before or since. He was just about unstoppable.

The Big Dipper (another nickname) led the NBA with 1,597 field goals during the 1961–1962 season. He also had the most free throws—835 in all. Add that up (and remember, FGs are worth 2 points each), and you get an all-time record 4,029 points. Do a little math (divide that by 80 games played), and your eyes might bug out: **CHAMBERLAIN *AVERAGED* 50.4 POINTS PER GAME FOR THE WHOLE SEASON!**

By comparison, there were only 13 games in 2017–2018 in which an individual player scored 50 or more points. The Big Dipper outdid them all by himself, by a long shot.

## Top 10 Single-Season Scoring Averages

| PLAYER, SEASON | AVG. |
|---|---|
| Wilt Chamberlain, 1961–62 | 50.4 |
| Wilt Chamberlain, 1962–63 | 44.8 |
| Wilt Chamberlain, 1960–61 | 38.4 |
| Wilt Chamberlain, 1959–60 | 37.6 |
| Michael Jordan, 1986–87 | 37.1 |
| Wilt Chamberlain, 1963–64 | 36.9 |
| Rick Barry, 1966–67 | 35.6 |
| Kobe Bryant, 2005–06 | 35.4 |
| Michael Jordan, 1987–88 | 35.0 |
| Kareem Abdul-Jabbar, 1971–72 | 34.9 |

# 73

In 1995–96, the Chicago Bulls won 72 games—the most by an NBA team for a single season. Led by Michael Jordan, the Bulls moved through the league like a steamroller, beating opponents in game after game. (They also won the NBA title that season.) Jordan led the league in scoring (again), helped by a team that included Scottie Pippen and sharpshooter Steve Kerr.

That was the standard for the Bulls at the time. A few teams threatened to match it, but no one really came that close.

Enter the Golden State Warriors.

Led by Stephen Curry and Klay Thompson, the Dubs crushed the competition during the 2015–16 season. They tied the Bulls with one more game to play against the Memphis Grizzlies. **THEY KNOCKED OUT THE GRIZZLIES 125–104 TO WIN NUMBER 73 AND SET A NEW NBA RECORD.**

One problem: The Warriors won 73 games in the season, but they were unable to win four games in the NBA Finals! LeBron James and the Cleveland Cavaliers spoiled the party by beating Golden State for the championship. At least Curry and Thompson will always have 73 wins!

**STEPHEN CURRY (LEFT) AND KLAY THOMPSON (RIGHT)**

## DIGIT-YOU-KNOW?

The WNBA version of the Warriors' record-setting season came in 2014. Led by supershooter Diana Taurasi, the Phoenix Mercury set the WNBA record with 29 wins. They lost only five games! No surprise here: They ended up as WNBA champs!

# 100

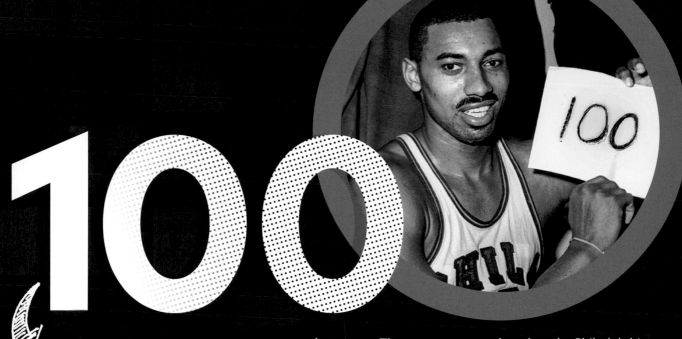

**W**e saw earlier that Wilt Chamberlain was a scoring machine. On March 2, 1962, he put a number of points on the scoreboard that no one has even gotten close to beating. This large, round, eye-popping, jaw-dropping number stunned the sports world. During the game, CHAMBERLAIN RACKED UP EXACTLY 100 POINTS, SETTING THE NBA SINGLE-GAME SCORING RECORD. And what's nearly as amazing is that so few people actually witnessed this pile-up of points.

The game was not played on the Philadelphia Warriors' home court. To cater to suburban fans, the team played a few contests in Hershey, Pennsylvania. Only a few thousand spectators caught the game (far fewer than those who saw Wilt play in Philly; the team's arena then held some 12,000 fans).

Wilt made 36 two-point shots for 72 points. He was a not a good free-throw shooter, but on this magic night he almost couldn't miss! He made 28 of his 32 one-point attempts. Add it up, and you've got an unbeatable record!

## NBA Top Five Single-Game Points Totals

| | |
|---|---|
| **100** | Wilt Chamberlain, Philadelphia Warriors, 1962 |
| **81** | Kobe Bryant, Los Angeles Lakers, 2006 |
| **78** | Wilt Chamberlain, Philadelphia Warriors, 1961 |
| **73** | David Thompson, Denver Nuggets, 1978 |
| **73** | Wilt Chamberlain, Philadelphia Warriors and San Francisco Warriors, 1962 |

KOBE BRYANT

## WNBA Top Single-Game Points Totals

LIZ CAMBAGE

| | |
|---|---|
| **53** | Liz Cambage, Dallas Wings, 2018 |
| **51** | Riquna Williams, Tulsa Shock, 2013 |
| **48** | Maya Moore, Minnesota Lynx, 2014 |
| **47** | Diana Taurasi, Phoenix Mercury, 2006 |
| **47** | Lauren Jackson, Seattle Storm, 2007 |
| **46** | Katie Smith, Minnesota Lynx, 2001 |

# 111

**T**he UCLA men's teams (page 114) and the Los Angeles Lakers (page 115) should just take a seat when the women's teams from the University of Connecticut enter the room. From 2014 to 2017, **THE UCONN HUSKIES WON 111 STRAIGHT GAMES.** It's the largest winning streak by any team, male or female, in any major college sport or professional sport.

They crushed just about everyone they played. The streak included a completely undefeated season (2015–16) and four national championships. But as you can see from the list of UConn national victories (right), winning the NCAA title is nothing new for the remarkable Huskies!

Thanks to the UConn student newspaper, *The Daily Campus,* here are some remarkable numbers from the streak of all streaks.

## STREAK NOTES

Number of days between UConn losses
**865 DAYS**

Number of games in which UConn won by at least 10 points
**108 GAMES**

Biggest margin of victory during the streak
(final score: 103–37 over South Florida)
**65 POINTS**

Closest margin of victory
(final score: 76–74 over Florida State)
**2 POINTS**

While this might look like a number for a whole team to score in a game, it was actually recorded on January 26, 1960, by one player: Danny Heater of West Virginia's Burnsville Bruins high school team. Wow.

# 135

Heater was the best player on the court. He and his teammates strategized for him to score as many points as possible, and score 'em he did. Heater made 53 out of 70 shots from the field. He added 29 free throws in 41 attempts. It helped his team to an easy 173–43 win over Widen High School.

Heater's feat remains the highest single-game total in U.S. high school hoops history.

## DIGIT-YOU-KNOW?

Here are the rest of the top five high school basketball single-game scoring totals.

| PLAYER | SCHOOL | YEAR | POINTS |
|---|---|---|---|
| Johnny Morris | Norcom High, Portsmouth, VA | 1961 | 127 |
| Dick Bogenrife | Midway High, Sedalia, OH | 1953 | 120 |
| Pete Cimino | Bristol High, Bristol, PA | 1960 | 114 |
| Wayne Oakley | Hanson High, Hanson, KY | 1954 | 114 |

## HISTORY
### BY THE NUMBERS

Cheryl Miller, who played for the USA Women's National Team and has served as a coach in the WNBA and NCAA, holds the record for most points scored in a women's high school game. She poured in 105 in a 1982 game. Lisa Leslie, who went on to play for the WNBA's Los Angeles Sparks, scored 101 points in the first half of a 1990 high school game. Her school's opponent refused to play the second half!

**Years the UConn's NCAA Women's Basketball team won championship titles**

| | | |
|---|---|---|
| 2016 | 2010 | 2002 |
| 2015 | 2009 | 2000 |
| 2014 | 2004 | 1995 |
| 2013 | 2003 | |

# 402

Stephen Curry made 286 three-point shots in the 2014–15 NBA season. No one had ever made that many. Steph had topped his own record by 14 and the record before that by 17. His total of 286 looked like a mark that would stand for a long time. But it didn't.

Curry stunned fans and opponents by destroying that record in the very next season. **THE LONG-RANGE SHOOTER BURIED AN ASTONISHING 402 THREES IN 2015–16.** That was a more than 40 percent jump. Imagine if someone beat the single-season home run record by that much—the stat would go from 73 to 102 runs! The most touchdowns by a player in a 16-game NFL season is 31. To achieve at least a 40 percent increase over that record, a football player would have to score 44 touchdowns!

## PENCIL POWER

How do we know that Curry's best record was 40 percent higher than the year before? Let's crunch the numbers! The year before he set his biggest record, Curry made 286 three-point shots. The next year he made 402, which was 116 more. Divide 116 by 286 and the result is .405, or just a little over 40 percent—402 is, therefore, slightly more than 40 percent higher than 286.

SETH CURRY

## STAT STORY

### A Family of Threes

Steph Curry's father Dell Curry had a long NBA career, from 1986 to 2002. He was also a great long-range shooter. Steph's younger brother, Seth, began his NBA career in 2013. Together, the Currys are the dominant three-point family.

*(Through 2019)*

| CURRY FAMILY MEMBER | CAREER THREE-POINTERS |
| --- | --- |
| Stephen Curry | 2,483 |
| Dell Curry | 1,245 |
| Seth Curry | 301 |

STEPHEN CURRY

DELL CURRY

When you're 7 feet 2 inches (2.2 m), you can already score over just about anyone. When Kareem Abdul-Jabbar added his signature skyhook shot to his game, he became just about unstoppable. **"THE BIG FELLA" HOLDS THE ALL-TIME NBA SCORING RECORD, WITH 38,387 POINTS.** A lot of them came on the skyhook, a one-handed flip from way above his head.

KAREEM ABDUL-JABBAR

# 38,387

Abdul-Jabbar had a great college career at UCLA, where he played under his birth name of Lew Alcindor. He eventually converted to the religion of Islam and changed his name. Abdul-Jabbar spent his first six pro seasons on the Milwaukee Bucks, winning two scoring titles, one NBA title, and three MVP awards. He joined the Lakers in 1975 and helped transform that team. Joining forces with Magic Johnson, he helped the Lakers win five NBA championships. He also won three more MVPs and added to his amazing streak of All-Star Games (during his career, Abdul-Jabbar appeared in 19 All-Star Games in all).

## DIGIT-YOU-KNOW?

Some players earn a whopping amount of points over the course of their careers, but points aren't the only career numbers that the NBA tracks. Here are some other notable four- and five-digit totals:

**CAREER ASSISTS**
John Stockton, 15,806

**CAREER BLOCKS**
Hakeem Olajuwon, 3,830

**CAREER REBOUNDS**
Wilt Chamberlain, 23,924

**CAREER STEALS**
John Stockton, 3,265

**CAREER FREE THROWS MADE**
Karl Malone, 9,787

**CAREER THREE-POINT SHOTS MADE**
Ray Allen, 2,973

# GLOSSARY

**alley-oop:** a pass that is lobbed near the rim for a teammate to slam home

**assist:** a pass that leads directly to a basket

**backspin:** the backward rotation of a ball

**bank shot:** a shot that bounces off the backboard and through the rim

**buzzer-beater:** a shot that goes in just as or just before the buzzer sounds, ending a quarter, half, or game

**clutch:** able to come through in the toughest situations when a team really needs it

**defense:** the act of preventing an opponent from scoring points in a game

**deuce:** a nickname for a two-point basket

**diameter:** the distance across the middle of a circle

**field goal:** any made basket that is not a free throw

**free throw:** a shot made from the free-throw line, awarded after certain fouls

**inbounds pass:** the throw that returns the ball to play after the ball goes out of bounds

**in the paint:** in the key, the area inside the free-throw lines

**key:** the rectangular area between the end line and the free-throw line

**layup:** a short shot dropped softly into the basket or bounced off the backboard from close range

**lob:** a high, arcing pass

**margin of victory:** the difference in points between the winning team and the losing team

**offense:** the act of trying to score points in a game

**parabola:** a U-shaped arc

**rebound:** a ball grabbed after any missed shot

**skyhook:** a type of shot made by raising one arm high above the head

**technical foul:** a penalty called on a player or coach for abusive language or rough play

**tip-off:** the play that begins a game or some restarts in play, when the referee tosses the ball up between two leaping players

**traction:** the adhesive friction between two bodies or objects

**trey:** nickname for a made three-point basket

**triple-double:** reaching double digits in three different stats in one game

**turnover:** losing the ball to the other team during play

## ABBREVIATIONS

**ABA:** American Basketball Association

**APG:** assists per game

**FIBA:** International Basketball Federation

**NBA:** National Basketball Association

**NCAA:** National Collegiate Athletic Association

**OT:** overtime

**PPG:** points per game

**RPG:** rebounds per game

**TO:** turnover or timeout

**WNBA:** Women's National Basketball Association

# INDEX

Illustrations are indicated by **boldface.**

# INDEX

# CREDITS

Unless otherwise noted, all illustrations: Kevin B. McFadin; cover: (UP RT), Boris Ryaposov/Adobe Stock; (stopwatch), Photodisc; (court), Auspicious/Shutterstock; (LO RT), Aaron Amat/Shutterstock; (LO LE), Dorling Kindersley/Getty Images; (whistle), Photo Melon/Shutterstock; (CTR LE), Alex Kravtsov/Shutterstock; (UP LE), mipan/Shutterstock; back cover (UP RT), Nuttanun/Adobe Stock; (chalkboard), mexrix/Shutterstock; (LO CTR), snaptitude/Adobe Stock; (CTR LE), Alex/Adobe Stock; 1, Aaron Amat/Shutterstock; 2, Dmitry Argunov/Shutterstock; 3, photomelon/Adobe Stock; 4-5, D Miralle/Getty Images; 6, Noah Graham/NBAE via Getty Images; 7, Chris Trotman/Getty Images; 9, Christian Petersen/Getty Images; 10-11, mhaprang/Adobe Stock; 11, Pictures Now/Alamy Stock Photo; 12-13, Vasilis Ververidis/Alamy Stock Photo; 12, Hy Peskin/Getty Images; 13, Andrew D. Bernstein/NBAE via Getty Images; 14 (UP), David Hahn/Icon Sportswire/Corbis via Getty Images; 14 (CTR RT), AP Photo/Mary Schwalm; 14 (LO), Tim Nwachukwu/NCAA Photos via Getty Images; 15 (LO), Icon Sportswire via AP Image; 16 (UP RT), Lorenzo Ciniglio/Sygma via Getty Images; 16 (hoop), EFKS/Shutterstock; 16 (Bol), B Bennett/Getty Images; 16 (James), Ezra Shaw/Getty Images; 16 (Naismith), Bettmann/Getty Images; 16 (girl), Ron Levine/Getty Images; 17 (UP RT), Hulton Archive/Getty Images; 17 (CTR LE), Shan Haijing/EPA/Shutterstock; 17 (LO RT), Ezra Shaw/Getty Images; 18 (ball), Aaron Amat/Shutterstock; 18 (tape), Vrabelpeter1/Dreamstime; 18 (chalk), Robyn Mackenzie/Shutterstock; 19, Javier Díez/Stocksy; 20, snaptitude/Adobe Stock; 21, Nuttanun/Adobe Stock; 22-23, Fernando Medina/NBAE via Getty Images; 23 (ball), Aaron Amat/Shutterstock; 24, Ryan McVay/Getty Images; 25 (UP), Photodisc; 25 (LO), Cal Sport Media via AP Images; 26 (LE), David Sherman/NBAE via Getty Image; 26 (RT), Scott W. Grau/Icon Sportswire via Getty Image; 27 (LE), Dylan Buell/Getty Images; 27 (RT), David E. Klutho/Sports Illustrated via Getty Images; 28 (CTR), Carl Skalak/Sports Illustrated via Getty Image; 28 (LO), Andrew D. Bernstein/NBAE via Getty Images; 29 (BACKGROUND), AP Photo/David J. Phillip; 29 (INSET), AP Photo/Stacy Bengs; 30-31, Adam Lacy/Icon Sportswire via AP Images; 30, AP Photo/Ron Schwane; 32 (CTR), PicturenetCorp/Adobe Stock; 32 (LO), 2Design/Adobe Stock; 33 (UP), wavebreak3/Adobe Stock; 33 (LO RT), Esbin-Anderson/Getty Images; 33 (LO LE), Photodisc; 34, Franck Camhi/Adobe Stock; 36, AP Photo; 37, Schulte Productions/Getty Images; 38 (UP), Jean-Francois Monier/AFP/Getty Image; 38 (LO), Matt A. Brown/Icon SMI/Icon Sport Media via Getty Images; 38 (Bird), Chris Poss/Alamy Live News; 38 (Curry), Cal Sport Media/Alamy Stock Photo; 39 (CTR), Andy Hayt/NBAE via Getty Images; 39 (RT), Chris Elise/Getty Images; 39 (Harden), Robert Laberge/Getty Images; 39 (Taurasi), Christian Petersen/Getty Images; 40 (LO LE), AP Photos/Lennox McLendon; 40 (CTR), Ron Hoskins/NBAE via Getty Images; 40 (James), AP Photo/Tony Dejak; 40 (Moore), Ron Waite/CSM/Alamy Live News; 41 (UP), Yoon S. Byun/Boston Globe via Getty Image; 41 (LO RT), Action Plus Sports Images/Alamy Stock Photo; 41 (Davis), Stephen Lew/CSM/Alamy Live News; 41 (Parker), Anthony Nesmith/Cal Sport Media/Alamy Stock Photo; 42 (LE), Jim Cummins/NBAE via Getty Images; 42 (RT), Anthony Nesmith/Cal Sport Media/Alamy Stock Photo; 42 (Cousins), Layne Murdoch/NBAE via Getty Images; 43 (UP), Icon Sportswire via AP Images; 43 (LO RT), AP Photo/Rick Scuteri; 43 (Bonner), AP Photo/Rick Scuteri; 43 (Sabonis), AP Photo/Darron Cummings; 44, Doug Pensinger/Getty Images; 45, AP Photo/Brandon Dill; 46 (9), Noah Graham/NBAE via Getty Images; 46 (24), Harry How/Getty Images; 46 (8), Jeff Gross/Getty Images; 46 (6), Everett Collection Historical/Alamy Stock Photo; 46 (00), Focus on Sport via Getty Images; 47 (James), Layne Murdoch/NBAE via Getty Images; 47 (Jordan), Bill Smith/NBAE/Getty Images; 47 (Moore), Cal Sport Media/Alamy Stock Photo; 47 (Bird), Focus on Sport/Getty Images; 47 (West), AP Photo/L.A. Times; 47 (CTR LE), Andrew D. Bernstein/NBAE via Getty Image; 48 (Muresan), Jon Hayt/NBAE via Getty Images; 48 (Dydek), Jed Jacobsohn/Getty Images; 48 (CTR), Focus on Sport/Getty Images; 48 (Bobbit), Noah Graham/NBAE via Getty Images; 49, Mitchell Leff/Getty Images; 50, Anton Rodionov/Shutterstock; 51 (UP), UK Athletics; 51 (LO), Y's harmony/Adobe Stock; 53, InfinityPhoto/Adobe Stock; 54, masisyan/Adobe Stock; 56 (UP), John McDonnell/The Washington Post via Getty Images; 56 (LO), Issouf Sanogo/AFP/Getty Images; 57 (UP), Fernando Medina/NBAE via Getty Images; 57 (LO), WavebreakMediaMicro/Adobe Stock; 58 (UP), Kevin Abele/Icon Sportswire via Getty Images; 58 (LO LE), Bernhard Lang/Getty Images; 58 (LO RT), M. Anthony Nesmith/Icon Sportswire via Getty Images; 59, Cal Sport Media/Alamy Stock Photo; 60 (LE), Randy Belice/NBAE via Getty Images; 60 (RT), Jevone Moore/Cal Sport Media/Alamy Stock Photo; 61 (LE), AP Photo/Seth Wenig; 61 (RT), Harry E. Walker/MCT via Getty Images; 62 (LE), cristovao31/Adobe Stock; 62 (ball), Aaron Amat/Shutterstock; 63 (UP), sergiy1975/Adobe Stock; 63 (LE), AP Photo; 63 (RT), NBA Photos/NBAE via Getty Images; 64-65, Brocreative/Shutterstock; 65 (UP), Jonathan Daniel/Getty Images; 65 (RT), Allen Einstein/NBAE/Getty Images; 66, Andrew D. Bernstein/NBAE via Getty Images; 67 (LE), Jed Jacobsohn/Getty Images; 67 (RT), AP Photo/Nell Redmond; 68 (UP), Adam Hunger/BIG3/Getty Images; 68 (LO), AP Photo/Orlin Wagner; 69, Catherine Steenkeste/NBAE via Getty Images; 71, Hraun/Getty Images; 72, Luis Louro/Adobe Stock; 74 (ball), Aaron Amat/Shutterstock; 74 (glass), Jalisko/Shutterstock; 74-75 (pebbles), bradcalkins/Adobe Stock; 75 (UP RT), Aaron Amat/Shutterstock; 75 (LO RT), Carlos Caetano/Adobe Stock; 75 (LO), Jeff Gross/Getty Image; 76, Gene Sweeney Jr./Getty Images/Getty Images; 77 (LE), Heritage Auctions, Dallas; 77 (RT), cristovao31/Adobe Stock; 78-79, AP Photo/Danny Karnik; 78 (UP), AP Photo; 78 (hoop), mipan/Shutterstock; 78 (balls), Aaron Amat/Shutterstock; 79, AP Photo/John Zeedick; 80-81, Gary Dineen/NBAE via Getty Images; 80 (LE), Hy Peskin/Getty Images; 80 (RT), David Ibinson/Alamy Stock Photo; 82 (1939), Everett Collection Inc/Alamy Stock Photo; 82 (1958), AP Photo/J. Walter Green; 82 (1973), AP Photo; 83 (1985), Jerry Wachter/Sports Illustrated via Getty Images; 83 (1997), Dimitri Iundt/Corbis/VCG via Getty Images; 83 (2019), David Dow/NBAE via Getty Images; 83 (LO RT), John W. McDonough/Sports Illustrated via Getty Images; 84-85 (ALL), Kaya Dengel, Yasemin Obuz, Selin Obuz; 86, Jacob Lund/Adobe Stock; 88 (UP RT), Ezra Shaw/Getty Images; 88 (CTR LE), AP Photo/Jim Mone; 88 (LO RT), AP Photo/Kathy Kmonicek; 89 (UP RT), Brad Horrigan/Hartford Courant/TNS via Getty Image; 89 (CTR LE), Fabrizio Andrea Bertani/Shutterstock; 89 (LO RT), Andy Lyons/Getty Images; 90, AP Photo/Elaine Thompson; 91 (LE), Dick Raphael/NBAE via Getty Images; 91 (LO), Ron Turenne/NBAE via Getty Images; 92 (UP), AP Photo; 92 (LE), George Tiedemann/Sports Illustrated via Getty Images; 93 (UP RT), Focus on Sport/Getty Images; 93 (CTR RT), AP Photo/Roy Dabner; 93 (LO RT), Jesse D. Garrabrant/NBAE via Getty Images; 93 (LO LE), Rocky Widner/NBAE via Getty Images; 93 (CTR LE), Larry W Smith/EPA/Shutterstock; 94 (UP), Layne Murdoch/NBAE via Getty Images; 94 (LO RT), Stephen Dunn/Getty Images; 94 (LO LE), Craig Jones/Getty Images; 95 (UP LE), John W. McDonough/Sports Illustrated via Getty Images; 95 (UP RT), Jim Cummins/NBAE via Getty Images; 95 (CTR RT), Focus on Sport/Getty Images; 95 (LO RT), Bill Baptist/WNBAE via Getty Image; 95 (LO LE), Heuler Andrey/Agif/Shutterstock; 95 (CTR LE), Nathaniel S. Butler/NBAE via Getty Image; 96 (CTR LE), AP Photo/Marcio Jose Sanchez; 96 (CTR RT), Focus on Sport/Getty Images; 96 (LO RT), Nathaniel S. Butler/NBAE via Getty Images; 97 (UP LE), Barry Gossage/NBAE via Getty Image; 97 (UP RT), David Blair/ZUMA Wire/Alamy Stock Photo; 97 (CTR RT), Jason Miller/Getty Images; 97 (LO RT), Jordan Johnson/NBAE via Getty Images; 97 (LO LE), P.A. Molumby/NBAE via Getty Image; 97 (CTR LE), Bill Baptist/NBAE via Getty Images; 98 (CTR LE), Focus on Sport/Getty Images; 98 (CTR RT), Christian Petersen/Getty Images; 98 (LO LE), AP Photo/Pete Leabo; 99 (UP LE), Bill Baptist/NBAE via Getty Images; 99 (UP RT), AP Photo/Eric Gay; 99 (CTR RT), Adam Pantozzi/NBAE via Getty Images; 99 (LO RT), Ethan Miller/Getty Image; 99 (LO LE), Joe Murphy/NBAE via Getty Images; 99 (CTR LE), AP Photo/Elise Amendola; 100 (UP RT), John W. McDonough/Sports Illustrated via Getty Images; 100 (CTR LE), Jason Miller/Getty Images; 100 (LO RT), Hannah Foslien/Getty Images; 101 (LE), AP Photo/Elise Amendola; 101 (RT), Drake University Archives & Special Collections; 102 (LE), Bill Baptist/NBAE via Getty Images; 102 (RT), Ned Dishman/NBAE via Getty Images; 103, AP Photo/Michael Conroy; 104-105, Dmytro Aksonov/Getty Images; 105 (maps), Ilya Kovshik/Shutterstock; 106 (UP LE), AP Photo/Mark LoMoglio; 106 (LO LE), AP Photo/Aaron Suozzi; 106 (LO RT), Photo by Streeter Lecka/Getty Images; 107, Juli Hansen/Shutterstock; 108-109 (paper), nicemonkey/Shutterstock; 108 (pens), vichly4thai/Adobe Stock; 108 (chalk), Robyn Mackenzie/Shutterstock; 108 (ball), Aaron Amat/Shutterstock; 108 (RT), Fuse/Getty Images; 109 (pencil), Yury Shirokov/Dreamstime; 109 (marker), IB Photography/Shutterstock; 110, master1305/Adobe Stock; 112-113 (ALL), Andrew D. Bernstein/NBAE via Getty Images; 114, Rich Clarkson/Sports Illustrated via Getty Images; 114 (ball), Aaron Amat/Shutterstock; 115 (UP), George Long/Sports Illustrated via Getty Images; 115 (logo), AP Photo; 115 (LO), AP Photo; 116 (LE), Stacy Revere/Getty Image; 116 (RT), AP Photo; 117, Herb Scharfman/Sports Illustrated via Getty Images; 118, Noah Graham/NBAE via Getty Images; 119 (UP), AP Photo/Paul Vathis; 119 (CTR), Noah Graham/NBAE via Getty Images; 119 (LO), Icon Sportswire via AP Images; 120, Cloe Poisson/Hartford Courant/TNS via Getty Images; 121 (UP), Yobro10/Dreamstime; 121 (LO), Heinz Kluetmeier/Walt Disney Television via Getty Images via Getty Images; 122 (LE), Elsa/Getty Images; 122 (CTR RT), Hector Acevedo/ZUMA Wire/Alamy Stock Photo; 122 (LO RT), Focus on Sport/Getty Images; 123, AP Photo/Reed Saxon

Since 1888, the National Geographic Society has funded more than 12,000 research, exploration, and preservation projects around the world. The Society receives funds from National Geographic Partners, LLC, funded in part by your purchase. A portion of the proceeds from this book supports this vital work. To learn more, visit natgeo.com/info.

NATIONAL GEOGRAPHIC and Yellow Border Design are trademarks of the National Geographic Society, used under license.

For more information, visit nationalgeographic.com, call 1-877-873-6846, or write to the following address:
National Geographic Partners
1145 17th Street N.W.
Washington, DC 20036-4688 U.S.A.

Visit us online at nationalgeographic.com/books

More for kids from National Geographic: natgeokids.com

*National Geographic Kids* magazine inspires children to explore their world with fun yet educational articles on animals, science, nature, and more. Using fresh storytelling and amazing photography, *Nat Geo Kids* shows kids ages 6 to 14 the fascinating truth about the world—and why they should care. **kids.nationalgeographic.com/subscribe**

For information about special discounts for bulk purchases, please contact National Geographic Books Special Sales: specialsales@natgeo.com

For rights or permissions inquiries, please contact National Geographic Books Subsidiary Rights: bookrights@natgeo.com

**Library of Congress Cataloging-in-Publication Data**
Names: Buckley, James, Jr., 1963- author.
Title: It's a numbers game : basketball / by Jim Buckley.
Other titles: Basketball
Description: Washington, DC : National Geographic Kids, 2020. I Series: It's a numbers game I Audience: Ages: 8–12. I Audience: Grades: 4–6.
Identifiers: LCCN 2019007821 I ISBN 9781426336898 (hardcover) I ISBN 9781426336904 (hardcover)
Subjects: LCSH: Basketball—Mathematics—Juvenile literature. I Mathematics—Study and teaching (Elementary)—Juvenile literature.
Classification: LCC GV885.1 .I87 2020 I DDC 796.323—dc23
LC record available at https://lccn.loc.gov/2019007821

This book is dedicated to the Wheezers, who helped me learn to play in our legendary Eastside vs Westside battles! And to my brother Tom and nephew Dalton, who love the game more than I do!

—JB Jr.

## EXPERT REVIEWERS

**Gail Burrill,** now in the Program in Mathematics Education at Michigan State University, was a secondary mathematics teacher for more than 28 years. She received the Presidential Award for Excellence in Teaching Mathematics, is a T3 National Instructor and elected member of the International Statistics Institute, and served as president of the National Council of Teachers of Mathematics and as president of the International Association of Statistical Education.

**Brenda Frese** has been the head coach of the University of Maryland women's basketball team for the past 17 seasons. She has helped lead the Terrapins to three Final Fours, six Elite Eights, eight Sweet Sixteens, 10 conference titles, and a National Championship in 2006. Frese has been named Conference Coach of the Year five times and was the 2002 Associated Press National Coach of the Year. Her program has a 100 percent graduation rate. She and her husband, Mark, have twin 11-year-old boys, Tyler and Markus.

Cover designed by Julide Dengel
Designed by Fan Works Design LLC

**National Geographic supports K–12 educators with ELA Common Core Resources. Visit natgeoed.org/commoncore for more information.**

The publisher would like to thank everyone who worked to make this book come together: Andrea Silen, project manager; Angela Modany, associate editor; Julide Dengel, art director/designer; Sarah J. Mock, senior photo editor; Robin Palmer, fact-checker; Sean Philpotts, production director; Sally Abbey, managing editor; Joan Gossett, editorial production manager; and Gus Tello and Anne LeongSon, design production assistants.

Printed in China
19/PPS/1